God's Economy:

The Tithe and New Testament Giving

Jeff Farris
© **2011**

Endless Journeys

ISBN: 978-0-9834774-0-2

Edited by Sandee Lloyd and Jeff Farris

All Scripture quotations are taken from the
King James Version of the Bible, provided by e-Sword
(www.e-sword.net © 2000-2009 Rick Meyers).

A special word of thanks:

To my brother/cousin Michael Redman who blazed this
trail ahead of me and provided some valuable information
toward self-publishing;

To the people at CreateSpace.com, who made self-
publishing an attainable goal for everyone;

To Sandee Lloyd, who painstakingly read through the first
manuscript, weeded out errors and provided rephrasing
for clarity;

To my lovely wife, Sarah, who enabled me to clean up
some of my, shall we say, more offensive comments? I
suppose that is why she is my better half.

Most of all, I thank my Lord and Savior, Jesus Christ;
who gave Himself for my sins. Without Him I could do
nothing.

Contents

3

God's Economy:

The Tithe
and
New Testament Giving

He that hath pity upon the poor lendeth unto the LORD; and
that which he hath given will he pay him again.

(Proverbs 19:17)

Preface

It was in January of 1980, at a First Christian Church down in Florida, that I accepted Jesus Christ and was baptized. I did not realize it at the time, but God had begun a work in my life that He would continue through the years to the end of my days.

I was barely in my twenties then, and had learned to love the night life. I liked to party with my buddies. We'd go to the bars and have beer parties and get involved in some questionable activities. Unfortunately, I continued in that way of life even after my salvation. For about three years I lived as if I had never met Christ. But I was not the same person on the inside. And while I did not understand the spiritual work going on in my soul, I did notice an increasing lack of pleasure in the things I once enjoyed.

During these three years, I worked various jobs ranging from orange grove irrigation to restaurant work. In every place I worked, I met other Christians. My new nature was attracted to these people, and they quickly became my friends. These Christians, from various denominations, believed things I had never heard about. Some of them used terms that were foreign to me, like "the rapture," and "sanctify." It was also common for them to argue their doctrinal differences with one another. My experiences with them led me to read the Bible to understand this new terminology. I also wanted to find out which church came closest to what the Bible taught. So I began to visit various churches as I read my Bible. It was during this time of taking in the Word of God that my life really began to take off, leaving my old ways and former buddies somewhere in the past.

As I visited the different churches and listened to the sermons, it seemed that sooner or later I would hear about this thing called the "tithe." It would either be the subject of an entire sermon, or it would find its way into sermons on other topics. I was informed that the tithe belonged to the Lord, and in order to fulfill my obligation to give God His tithe, ten percent of my income was to be given to the church; before taxes. This immediately conflicted with the way I understood salvation. I was originally led to believe that salvation was a free gift. Now it appeared that someone had put a price tag on it (in dollars and cents).

Of course, I knew that the preacher had to be paid, and that there were other expenses related to the church building and the different ministries, so it made sense to give an offering. But I did not like what I was hearing. It seemed to contradict what I had been taught about Jesus and the grace of God. Yet it was being preached by so many, and even the seemingly more mature Christians spoke in favor of it. Some people even had testimonies about how God had helped them through a financial crisis after they gave their tithe.

One evening, I got with a Christian friend, and we studied the topic in order to find out what the New Testament had to say about tithing. Using a *Strong's Exhaustive Concordance,* we checked every New Testament passage we could find on the subject. We found nothing in the New Testament about giving a tithe to the church. In those days I was also a faithful listener of gospel radio. One renowned radio preacher of those years, Dr. J. Vernon McGee, on his *Thru the Bible Radio* broadcast, taught that the tithe was for the Old Testament but not for today.[1] Yet local preachers in the

---

[1] See also McGee, J. Vernon, *Through the Bible with J. Vernon McGee*, Vol. V, p. 128. Pasadena, CA, Through the Bible Radio, 1983.

churches I attended continued to teach that the tithe was God's standard for giving to the church, and they backed up their words with Scripture.

For over twenty-five years of my Christian experience, I have heard arguments from all sides. I've been to college and took classes on the Bible, and I've been to seminary for deeper biblical study. Some of my teachers assumed the tithe to be God's standard for giving. Others did not agree. To this day, preachers continue to demand the tithe, while others teach the opposite. At best, the subject is controversial. As such, it hardly falls under the category of sound doctrine. As a pastor, I could never bring myself to impose this questionable doctrine onto my congregation.

For the sake of my own conscience, I committed myself to thoroughly study the tithe of the Bible to more accurately understand what it was all about. I also researched the New Testament to learn what Christ and his apostles taught regarding giving and support for the ministry. The result of that study led to this work, and I have to admit that I found it disturbing to learn God's intended purpose for His tithe, while knowing how the tithe is taught and used in churches today. I found it no less disturbing to learn the New Testament's instructions on giving; because much of what is accepted and taught in this area today, and is also passed off as Bible truth, has practically nothing in common with God's original intent as revealed through His Word in regard to giving.

There is a difference between what the Scriptures teach, and how they are being used today to teach something that God never intended. And the frustrating part about the whole thing is that this modern paradigm of tithes and offerings is so well established that to speak out against it is viewed as almost blasphemous. Yet the truth is what it is, and so I humbly submit this work, and let the chips fall where they may. But please consider carefully what you read in this book. It is the result of over twenty years of experience and honest research. Here you will find the secrets of God's blessings openly revealed, as well as a formula for disaster. That our current trend has favored disaster is evident in our present economical situation.

I close this preface with a caution and a challenge. By its very nature, this topic is highly volatile; for it concerns the livelihood of ministers and their families. It also carries with it a threat of defunding many of today's accepted church practices. Indeed, some things will be overturned, as Jesus did the tables of the money-changers in the Temple (Matt. 21:12-13). And while pastoral support is biblical, a luxurious lifestyle at congregational expense is not. Consequently, some will find this work very offensive. However, I would challenge anyone with an honest heart, especially church leaders, to seriously look into the things addressed in this book with the understanding that we are confronting the Word of God. We do not take that lightly.

In submitting this, I understand that I am a mere human, capable of flying off the handle over small things. But before you blow me off as some radical religious nut making a mountain out of a molehill, again, please consider: If I, a mere human am disturbed at what I see as a blatant disregard for human provision in favor of choir robes, organs, television shows, and cathedrals, how much more might God not be well pleased?

Introduction

Many churches teach that God's standard for giving to the ministry is the tithe, meaning that ten percent of one's income is to be given to the church. Using passages from the Old Testament, it is taught that as God expected Israel to tithe, He expects Christians to tithe as well.

Where did this idea of tithing to God come from? Why did God command Israel to tithe? Who among the Israelites were required to tithe, and what items were they supposed to give? God directed that certain people would receive these tithes. Who were these people and why should they receive the tithes of someone else's labor? What does the New Testament say about the tithe? How are Christians supposed to give according to New Testament teachings?

As the title suggests, this work seeks to provide a thorough understanding of the tithe and New Testament giving according to their purpose in God's economy. From Genesis to Deuteronomy, we will study the origin of the tithe and learn how it became incorporated into God's covenant with Israel. An examination of the historical books of the Old Testament will reveal how the Israelites understood and carried out God's instructions. From the prophetic books we will find out how the tithe played a role in Israel's unfaithfulness to God, inviting His punishment. Scriptures will be examined for context, with final analyses that will include comparisons to modern concepts of tithing.

The New Testament will be examined in regard to the tithe and giving. We will read what Jesus taught, and how the early disciples understood His words. From the epistles of the New Testament, we will learn the apostles' doctrine on giving as inspired by the Holy Spirit.

An appendix has been added as a supplement to aid our understanding of how church doctrine on giving developed and changed over the centuries. Primary sources here include writings from the earliest Church Fathers, as well as the official canons of various church councils throughout the Middle-Ages.

It is the hope of this work to correct some misconceptions and falsehoods regarding the tithe and Christian giving. It is also a hope of this work to lighten the burden for Christians who struggle financially. Finally, this is written with the hope that we will understand God's ownership of all things, including ourselves, so that He might have full access to every area of our lives for His purpose and glory, according as He has enabled each of us.

Part I

The Tithe

Chapter 1

The Tithe before the Law

There are two instances where the tithe occurs in the Old Testament before the Law of Moses. The first is in the life of Abraham and the second involved Jacob. This presence of the tithe so early in Scripture has led some Bible scholars to elevate its significance to something very near and dear to God. Because of this understanding, they hold that the tithe has always been God's standard for giving throughout the ages.

On the other hand, early traditions reveal that tithing was associated with idol worship,[2] which could easily have contributed to the cultural influence leading to Abraham's tithe, or Jacob's promise to return the tenth of God's blessing. It was also the practice of kings to demand tithes from their subjects (1st Sam. 8:10-17).[3] As Abraham and Jacob lived in that world, they would certainly have been familiar with these practices (Gen. 35:2-4; Josh. 24:2).

Genesis 14:18-20: Abraham's Tithe

The first tithe recorded in the Bible is found in Genesis chapter 14. The text relates an account of servitude and rebellion in ancient times. The king of Elam had subjugated the city of Sodom along with four other cities. They served him for twelve years, and in the thirteenth year they rebelled (14:1-14). It is highly probable that this

---

[2]   Philip Schaff, ed. *Schaff-Herzog Encyclopædia of Religious Knowledge*, Vol. IV (New York: Funk & Wagnalls Co., 1891), p. 2365. Hereafter referred to as *Schaff-Herzog*. See also Henry Lansdell D.D., *The Sacred Tenth, or Studies in Tithe-Giving, Ancient and Modern*, pp. 12-16 (New York: 1906). Hereafter referred to as *The Sacred Tenth*.

[3]   See also William Benton, publisher: *Encyclopaedia Britannica*, Vol. 22, pp. 252-253, "Tithes." (Chicago: Encyclopaedia Britannica, Inc., 1959).

king was demanding their tithes.

In the fourteenth year, the king of Elam and his allies waged war with these cities, defeating and plundering them. Abram's nephew Lot, who lived in Sodom, was among those who had been taken captive (14:5-12). Upon learning of Lot's capture, Abram and 318 armed men pursued Lot's captors and gained the victory over them. Lot was rescued, and all that was taken was restored (14:12-16). It is at this point we are introduced to a king-priest named Melchizedek, and the first recorded tithe in the Bible.

> **Genesis 14:18-20**
> **[14:18] And Melchizedek king of Salem brought forth bread and wine: and he *was* the priest of the most high God. [19] And he blessed him, and said, Blessed *be* Abram of the most high God, possessor of heaven and earth: [20] And blessed be the most high God, which hath delivered thine enemies into thy hand. And he [Abram]⁴ gave him [Melchizedek] tithes of all.**

In this first instance of the tithe, we find Abram giving a tenth of the spoils of battle to a priest named Melchizedek. This was apparently a free-will offering on Abram's part, as there is nothing in the text of a command from God, nor anything from Melchizedek requiring it of him. Note also the sequence of events. The offering was given after Abram had defeated the enemy and obtained the spoils, and after he received the bread, wine, and the blessing from the priest. Other than this passage, we have no further Scriptural evidence of Abram, or Abraham as he is later called, paying the tithe.

The fact that Abram returned victorious and was met by the man of God was providential. What happened during that battle we do not know, but the verification by

---

⁴ The names were inserted to clear up any immediate textual confusion that may be caused by the pronouns (he, him). See also Hebrews 7:1-2.

Melchizedek that God delivered the enemy into Abram's hand likely confirmed the situation as experienced by Abram. Acknowledgement to the truth of Melchizedek's words is seen in Abram's offering. It appears that Abram knew all too well that the victory was not his own.

There is a lesson to be learned here, but the item (the tithe) is not the issue. The lesson for us is the right attribution of glory. Peter and John exemplified it at the temple, upon healing the lame beggar.

Acts 3:11-16

[3:11] And as the lame man which was healed held Peter and John, all the people ran together unto them in the porch that is called Solomon's, greatly wondering. [12]And when Peter saw *it*, he answered unto the people, Ye men of Israel, why marvel ye at this? Or why look ye so earnestly on us, as though by our own power or holiness we had made this man to walk? [13] The God of Abraham, and of Isaac, and of Jacob, the God of our fathers, hath glorified his Son Jesus; whom ye delivered up, and denied him in the presence of Pilate, when he was determined to let *him* go. [14] But ye denied the Holy One and the Just, and desired a murderer to be granted unto you; [15] and killed the Prince of life, whom God hath raised from the dead; whereof we are witnesses. [16] And his name through faith in his name hath made this man strong, whom ye see and know: yea, the faith which is by him hath given him this perfect soundness in the presence of you all.

Peter and John had nothing whereof to glory, but in Christ. It was through the name of Jesus that the lame man was healed. They proclaimed His glory to all the people. In like manner, Abram had nothing whereof to glory, but in the LORD who delivered the enemy into his hand. Abram demonstrated honesty in character by glorifying God through acknowledging the truth of Melchizedek's proclamation. This lesson of right attribution of glory is repeated throughout Scripture: let those who glory, glory in the Lord.

1 Corinthians 1:26-31

[1:26] For ye see your calling, brethren, how that not many wise men after the flesh, not many mighty, not many noble, *are called*: [27] But God hath chosen the foolish things of the world to confound the wise; and God hath chosen the weak things of the world to confound the things which are mighty; [28] And base things of the world, and things which are despised, hath God chosen, *yea*, and things which are not, to bring to nought things that are: [29] That no flesh should glory in his presence. [30] But of him are ye in Christ Jesus, who of God is made unto us wisdom, and righteousness, and sanctification, and redemption: [31] that, according as it is written, He that glorieth, let him glory in the Lord.

Ephesians 2:8-9

[2:8] For by grace are ye saved through faith; and that not of yourselves: *it is* the gift of God: [9] not of works, lest any man should boast.

If attributing glory to kings or gods in Abram's time meant offering tithes, then Abram rightly attributed glory to God in the sight of the people present. In the context of Peter and John's experience, they rightly deflected glory from themselves by directing the focus of the people's faith toward Jesus Christ.

The lesson here is not about whether or not you are paying tithes to the church; but rather, how we can attribute glory to Jesus Christ in no uncertain terms and be an effective witness to those around us.

Genesis 28:10-22: Jacob's Tenth

The second occurrence of the "tenth" in Scripture is in Genesis 28, where we find Jacob running for his life. This story actually begins in Chapter 27, where Jacob deceived his blind and aging father, Isaac. Following his mother Rebecca's instructions, Jacob pretended to be his brother Esau, and effectively tricked his father into giving him

Esau's blessing (27:1-30). Esau quickly discovered what Jacob had done, but knew nothing of Rebecca's involvement. Responding in anger, Esau planned to kill Jacob (27:30-41). Rebecca learned of this plot and warned Jacob to flee for his safety. She made arrangements with Isaac for Jacob's departure, under the pretense that Jacob would go away to get a wife from their homeland. (27:42-28:5). It is in this context, with Jacob fleeing for his life, that we have the following account:

Genesis 28:10-22

[28:10] And Jacob went out from Beersheba, and went toward Haran. [11] And he lighted upon a certain place, and tarried there all night, because the sun was set; and he took of the stones of that place, and put *them for* his pillows, and lay down in that place to sleep. [12] And he dreamed, and behold a ladder set up on the earth, and the top of it reached to heaven: and behold the angels of God ascending and descending on it. [13] And, behold, the LORD stood above it, and said, I *am* the LORD God of Abraham thy father, and the God of Isaac: the land whereon thou liest, to thee will I give it, and to thy seed; [14] And thy seed shall be as the dust of the earth, and thou shalt spread abroad to the west, and to the east, and to the north, and to the south: and in thee and in thy seed shall all the families of the earth be blessed. [15] And, behold, I *am* with thee, and will keep thee in all *places* whither thou goest, and will bring thee again into this land; for I will not leave thee, until I have done *that* which I have spoken to thee of.

[28:16] And Jacob awaked out of his sleep, and he said, "Surely the LORD is in this place; and I knew *it* not." [17] And he was afraid, and said, "How dreadful *is* this place! This *is* none other but the house of God, and this *is* the gate of heaven." [18] And Jacob rose up early in the morning, and took the stone that he had put *for* his pillows, and set it up *for* a pillar, and poured oil upon the top of it. [19] And he called the name of that place Bethel: but the name of that city *was called* Luz at the first. [20] And Jacob vowed a vow, saying, "If God will be with me, and will keep me in this way that I go, and will give me bread to eat, and raiment to put on, [21] So that I come again to my father's house in peace; then shall the LORD be my God: [22] And this stone, which I have set *for* a pillar, shall be God's house: and of all that thou shalt give me I will surely give the tenth unto thee."

This is the second appearance of the tithe (or tenth) in Scripture, and it is Jacob who mentions it. There is nothing in this passage to imply that the LORD required this of him. Quite to the contrary, God had made an open ended promise to Jacob without demanding, or even suggesting anything in return (28:13-15). Jacob, however, made a vow to God, promising to return a tenth of God's blessing *after* God fulfilled His part (28:20-22).

Regarding this vow, we have no passage from Scripture indicating that Jacob ever did what he said he was going to do. But neither did the LORD give to Jacob the land that He promised to him. Jacob's life ended in Egypt (Genesis 47-50). Yet as we study the passage in detail, we see that God's promise was not to Jacob alone. The promise was to Jacob *and his seed*. Note also that the LORD bound Jacob with his descendants into a single unit: "***thy seed* shall be as the dust..., and *thou* shalt spread abroad....**" (28:13-14). Jacob did not fulfill his vow to return that tenth because God's promise was not fulfilled in his lifetime. It is significant at this point to note that in Genesis 32:28, God gave Jacob a new name: Israel. And it was not until after the deliverance of Israel and their exodus from Egypt that God required the tithe that Jacob had vowed. In making this vow at Bethel, Jacob (as the head of his progeny), began what would ultimately become the tithe of Israel.

The Tithe before the Law: Final Analysis

Abraham

Advocates for the modern doctrine of tithing point out that tithing occurred *before* the Law, and Abraham is used as an example. Like Abraham before the Law, Christians are justified by faith apart from the Law (Romans 3:21; 4:13, 16; 5:1; Gal. 3:8-9). Since Abraham paid the tithe, so the argument goes, we are to follow his example. While human logic and reasoning may lead to such a conclusion, the Scriptures do not tell us that.

One obvious problem with this argument is that Abraham tithed one time. He tithed of the spoils of battle. There is no Scriptural evidence that God required this of him, making this is a free-will offering. Nor is there any evidence that Abraham ever tithed again. Abraham's one time free-will offering is hardly a basis to exact a ten percent tribute of one's regular income.

The sequence of events in Abraham's tithe is of particular interest. It is often said that God will bless us *after* we first give the tenth. In other words, our financial blessings from God are contingent upon our tithing to Him first (this argument is based on a partial reading of Malachi 3). But that is not how it worked with Abraham. Abraham received the victory. He received the spoils of battle. He received his nephew back. He received the bread, wine and blessing from God's priest *before* he gave the tithe. It would appear that if Abraham is to be our example, then the blessing should come first. But again, the lesson in Abraham's tithe is not about tithing as we know it. The lesson is one of rightly attributed glory, and that can be done in any number of ways.

Jeremiah 9:23-24

[9:23] Thus saith the LORD, Let not the wise *man* glory in his wisdom, neither let the mighty *man* glory in his might, let not the rich *man* glory in his riches: [24] But let him that glorieth glory in this, that he understandeth and knoweth me, that I *am* the LORD which exercise lovingkindness, judgment, and righteousness, in the earth: for in these *things* I delight, saith the LORD.

Jacob

Like Abraham, Jacob is also cited as one who knew to tithe to God before the Law of Moses was written. The footnotes in *The Believer's Study Bible* go so far as to suggest that this act of Jacob confirmed tithing as a "godly practice."[5] The *Bible Knowledge Commentary* calls Jacob's promise to give the tenth, as well as Abraham's tithe a "motif,"[6] thus elevating the tithe to a position of special recognition. As with Abraham, we are instructed to follow Jacob's godly example and pay the tithe.

However, the circumstances surrounding this occasion would more likely lead to an opposite conclusion; and so we ask the question. Is Jacob really a commendable example to be followed at this juncture in his life? He lied to his father to the extent of taking the name of the LORD in vain (Gen. 27:20). He stole from his brother, and was running for his life. At this time in his life, Jacob was a lying thief on the run. In this passage, he had vowed to God not only that he would return the tenth to God *if* God would take care of him, but he also stated that the LORD would be his God *after* he received the promises of God. In other words, Jacob said, "*If* you do all of this that I ask,

---

[5] W. A. Criswell, Ph. D. ed., *The Believer's Study Bible*, Luke 11:42 note (Thomas Nelson Publishers, Nashville, 1991), p. 1461.

[6] John F. Walvoord and Roy B. Zuck, eds., *The Bible Knowledge Commentary: Old Testament* (Victor Books, Wheaton, IL, 1985), p. 74. Hereafter referred to as Walvoord and Zuck.

then you will be my God." Or to put it in the negative, "You are not my God now, but do all of this for me and you will be." Unlike Abraham, who merely accepted God's promises and believed God, Jacob's lack of trust is revealed in his "*if* you do this, *then* I will do that" attitude.

The LORD did not require Jacob's tithe. It was Jacob's own idea. Rather than view Jacob as a role model in this situation, his rash reaction to the unexpected presence of God probably compares better with Peter's misguided idea to build three tabernacles during the transfiguration of Jesus Christ (Matthew 17:1-5). Regarding such things as vows, the best advice can be found in these words of Jesus:

Matthew 5:33-37

[5:33] Again, ye have heard that it hath been said by them of old time, Thou shalt not forswear thyself, but shalt perform unto the Lord thine oaths: [34] But I say unto you, Swear not at all; neither by heaven; for it is God's throne: [35] Nor by the earth; for it is his footstool: neither by Jerusalem; for it is the city of the great King. [36] Neither shalt thou swear by thy head, because thou canst not make one hair white or black. [37] But let your communication be, Yea, yea; Nay, nay: for whatsoever is more than these cometh of evil.

Jacob only had to say, "Yes!" God had promised to him and to his descendants an open-ended promise. He had only to receive it. But Jacob did not do that, and according to what Jesus said, Jacob's response was evil in its origin. This is no worthy example, by any stretch of the imagination.

God made a promise to Jacob, and He also made some promises to us: "Believe in Jesus Christ and you shall be saved" (Acts 16:31). "Whoever shall call upon the name of the Lord shall be saved" (Romans 10:13). "Confess with your mouth the Lord Jesus and believe in your heart that God raised Him from the dead and you will be saved" (Romans 10:9).

Salvation is a free gift. It has no price tag. It is totally undeserved, and is based on the goodness of God and His great love which He has for us. It does not nor will not depend anything we have done or can do (Ephesians 2:8-9). Receive the promise. It is an open-ended promise to eternal life, and it is free.

Chapter 2

The Tithe According to the Law

The Law begins with God's commandments to Israel through the mediation of Moses, and runs from Exodus 20 to the end of Deuteronomy. For our purpose, Leviticus, Numbers and Deuteronomy provide the specifics regarding the tithe and its use in God's economy under the Law. Leviticus details what was tithed and how the tithe was chosen. In Numbers we understand how the tithe was used during Israel's years in the wilderness, while Deuteronomy looks beyond the wandering years to life in the Promised Land, with different instructions for tithing.

Leviticus 27:30-34: God Claims His Tithe

The first occurrence of the tithe according to the Law is found at the end of the Book of Leviticus. Leviticus 27 deals with vows made to the LORD (27:2). Recall that in Genesis 28, God promised to give the land to Jacob and his descendants. In response, Jacob had vowed to return a tenth of all that the LORD would give him. It is in this section dealing with vows that the LORD rightly claims what has been vowed, as He fulfills His promise in the giving of the land. This is the first time that God personally mentions the tithe.

> **Leviticus 27:30-34**
> [27:30] And all the tithe of the land, *whether* of the seed of the land, *or* of the fruit of the tree, *is* the LORD'S: *it is* holy unto the LORD. [31] And if a man will at all redeem *ought* of his tithes, he shall add thereto the fifth *part* thereof. [32] And concerning the tithe of the herd, or of the flock, *even of* whatsoever passeth under the rod, the tenth shall be holy unto the LORD. [33] He shall not search whether it be good

or bad, neither shall he change it: and if he change it at all, then both it and the change thereof shall be holy; it shall not be redeemed. [34] These *are* the commandments, which the LORD commanded Moses for the children of Israel in Mount Sinai.

Note that the statement, **"all the tithe…, is the LORD'S**," is not an open ended statement to be applied to everything and everybody. It is an exclusive statement that is made here, applicable only to the children of Israel (27:34). Note also that there are only two areas in which the LORD required the tithe. The first is the **"tithe of the land"** (27:30). This would be the produce: **"the seed of the land, or the fruit of the tree**." The LORD also required a **"tithe of the herd, or of thy flock"** (27:32). Remember that Jacob had vowed to return a tenth of all that God would give him. The land is what God had promised, and Israel was about to receive that. Jacob also credited God for providing his livestock (Gen. 31:9), so it must be tithed as well. God did not demand anything from Israel outside of what Jacob had vowed. Thus, the tithe was exclusive to produce and livestock. Everything else was exempt. Fish and other marine creatures were not tithed, nor were handcrafted items, precious stones or money.

Of the items that were tithed, only produce could be redeemed (27:31, 33). Regarding livestock, the tithe was not taken from the first or the best. It was the tenth animal that **"passeth under the rod"** that was to be tithed. The condition of the animal, **"whether it be good or bad**," was not a consideration in this selection (27:32-33). If the tenth animal was sick, blemished, or weak, it was tithed. If the tenth was young, healthy and spotless, it was tithed. And since it was the tenth that passed under the rod, if one owned twenty-nine sheep, only two would be tithed as there would be no tenth in the third group to pass under the rod.

While these instructions include what was tithed, what was redeemable and the cost of redemption, there is no mention as to who would receive the tithe or how the tithe was used. The final statement is clear that these commandments were specifically **"for the children of Israel"** (27:34).

Numbers 18:24-32: The Tithe in the Wandering Years

The next place we find the tithe is in the book of Numbers. In Leviticus God claimed His tithe. He described what was to be tithed, and how the tithe was selected. In Numbers we begin to understand how God's tithe was first put to use.

> **Numbers 18:24-32**
> [18:24] But the tithes of the children of Israel, which they offer *as* an heave offering unto the LORD, I have given to the Levites to inherit: therefore I have said unto them, Among the children of Israel they shall have no inheritance. [25] And the LORD spake unto Moses, saying, [26] Thus speak unto the Levites, and say unto them, When ye take of the children of Israel the tithes which I have given you from them for your inheritance, then ye shall offer up an heave offering of it for the LORD, *even* a tenth *part* of the tithe. [18:27] And *this* your heave offering shall be reckoned unto you, as though *it were* the corn of the threshingfloor, and as the fulness of the winepress. [28] Thus ye also shall offer an heave offering unto the LORD of all your tithes, which ye receive of the children of Israel; and ye shall give thereof the LORD'S heave offering to Aaron the priest. [29] Out of all your gifts ye shall offer every heave offering of the LORD, of all the best thereof, *even* the hallowed part thereof out of it. [30] Therefore thou shalt say unto them, When ye have heaved the best thereof from it, then it shall be counted unto the Levites as the increase of the threshingfloor, and as the increase of the winepress. [31] And ye shall eat it in every place, ye and your households: for it *is* your reward for your

service in the tabernacle of the congregation. [32] And ye shall bear no sin by reason of it, when ye have heaved from it the best of it: neither shall ye pollute the holy things of the children of Israel, lest ye die.

While Leviticus details what was tithed, here in Numbers we learn that God used it to feed the Levites, for they had no inheritance (18:24). They served in the tabernacle, and the tithe was their reward for service there (18:31). Note that the Levites were also required to tithe. They were to give a tenth of the tithe they collected from Israel as an offering to the LORD (18:26). This tithe was to go to Aaron the priest (18:28) and consisted of grain and wine (18:27, 30). Because of the warning attached to these instructions, it was imperative that the Levites tithed their very best (18:32).

Deuteronomy 12:1, 5-12, 17-19: The Tithe in the Land

Here we find that the instructions about the tithe are different from those in the book of Numbers. This is because the instructions in Numbers were for Israel as they wandered in the desert. Deuteronomy contains the statutes they would observe once they were settled in the land.

Deuteronomy 12:1, 5-14, 17-19
[12:1] These *are* the statutes and judgments, which ye shall observe to do in the land, which the LORD God of thy fathers giveth thee to possess it, all the days that ye live upon the earth.

[12:5] But unto the place which the LORD your God shall choose out of all your tribes to put his name there, *even* unto his habitation shall ye seek, and thither thou shalt come: [6] And thither ye shall bring your burnt offerings, and your sacrifices, and your tithes, and heave offerings of your hand, and your vows, and your freewill offerings, and the firstlings of your herds and of your flocks: [7] And there ye shall eat before the LORD your God, and ye shall rejoice in all that ye put your hand unto, ye and your households, wherein the LORD thy God hath blessed thee.

[8] Ye shall not do after all *the things* that we do here this day, every man whatsoever *is* right in his own eyes. [9] For ye are not as yet come to the rest and to the inheritance, which the LORD your God giveth you. [10] But *when* ye go over Jordan, and dwell in the land which the LORD your God giveth you to inherit, and *when* he giveth you rest from all your enemies round about, so that ye dwell in safety; [11] Then there shall be a place which the LORD your God shall choose to cause his name to dwell there; thither shall ye bring all that I command you; your burnt offerings, and your sacrifices, your tithes, and the heave offering of your hand, and all your choice vows which ye vow unto the LORD: [12] And ye shall rejoice before the LORD your God, ye, and your sons, and your daughters, and your menservants, and your maidservants, and the Levite that *is* within your gates; forasmuch as he hath no part nor inheritance with you. [13] Take heed to thyself that thou offer not thy burnt offerings in every place that thou seest: [14] But in the place which the LORD shall choose in one of thy tribes, there thou shalt offer thy burnt offerings, and there thou shalt do all that I command thee.

[12:17] Thou mayest not eat within thy gates the tithe of thy corn, or of thy wine, or of thy oil, or the firstlings of thy herds or of thy flock, nor any of thy vows which thou vowest, nor thy freewill offerings, or heave offering of thine hand: [18] But thou must eat them before the LORD thy God in the place which the LORD thy God shall choose, thou, and thy son, and thy daughter, and thy manservant, and thy maidservant, and the Levite that *is* within thy gates: and thou shalt rejoice before the LORD thy God in all that thou puttest thine hands unto. [19] Take heed to thyself that thou forsake not the Levite as long as thou livest upon the earth.

This passage clearly states that these instructions are different from what the Israelites had been doing. Verse 8 denotes a change; whatever they had been doing would come to an end: **"Ye shall not do after all the things that we do here this day"** (12:8). The rest of that verse, **"every man whatsoever is right in his own eyes"** is unclear. It might be that some details not covered specifically under God's instructions were left open to individual interpretation. Or perhaps they had already departed from God's original instructions. Whatever the case, we are to understand that the system of tithing, as well as the way they performed other offerings during the years of wandering would come to a close, and the instructions here in Deuteronomy were to be followed once they settled **"in the land"** (12:1).

Upon settlement in the land, God would choose a specific place and cause His name to dwell there (12:5, 11, 14, 18). All sacrifice and offering would be brought to this place. Unlike the Book of Numbers, which details a distribution of tithes to the Levites, with a tenth of the tithe from the Levites to Aaron, Deuteronomy allows everyone to partake of their tithes and offerings: **"ye and all your households"** (12:7); **"ye, your sons, and your daughters, and your menservants, and your maidservants, and the Levite that is within your gates"** (12:12, 18). This was to be a time of **"rest and the inheritance"** for Israel (12:9). It was a time of celebration for all of God's people; one big family cookout! The differences between Israel's years of wandering and God's plan for their life in the Promised Land are evident in these passages.

While everyone was invited to take part in all that was offered, including the tithe, the Levites were not to be forsaken (12:19). Once the party and celebration was finished, the Levites still needed support. After the feasting, there would be plenty left of the tithes and offerings for the priests and Levites who stayed to minister at the tabernacle (2nd Chron. 31:10). They would also continue to receive the regular offerings throughout the year (Deut. 18:1-8); but what about the other Levites?

Unlike the book of Numbers, which provided instruction for the tribes of Israel that were separated into different camps unto themselves (Num. 2), these instructions look forward to a situation in which Levites would be living throughout the Land among the people; hence the phrase, **"the Levite that is within thy gates"** (12:12, 18). Each community would now be responsible for the care of the Levites who lived among them. It would no longer be practical to continue tithing according to the book of Numbers.

Note that there is no mention of a frequency for tithing in this passage. There is a reason for omitting it at this point, as we shall see.

Deuteronomy 14:22-29: The Tithe in the Land, Continued

In this next section of Deuteronomy we find further instructions about the new system of tithing. The question of traveling a long distance with a large load is settled here, as well as some specifics in caring for the Levites.

> Deuteronomy 14:22-29
> [14:22] Thou shalt truly tithe all the increase of thy seed that the field bringeth forth year by year. [23] And thou shalt eat before the LORD thy God, in the place which he shall choose to place his name there, the tithe of thy corn, of thy wine, and of thine oil, and the firstlings of thy herds and of thy flocks; that thou mayest learn to fear the LORD thy God always.
> [14:24] And if the way be too long for thee, so that thou art not able to carry it; *or* if the place be too far from thee, which the LORD thy God shall choose to set his name there, when

the LORD thy God hath blessed thee: [25] Then shalt thou turn *it* into money, and bind up the money in thine hand, and shalt go unto the place which the LORD thy God shall choose: [26] And thou shalt bestow that money for whatsoever thy soul lusteth after, for oxen, or for sheep, or for wine, or for strong drink, or for whatsoever thy soul desireth: and thou shalt eat there before the LORD thy God, and thou shalt rejoice, thou, and thine household, [27] And the Levite that *is* within thy gates; thou shalt not forsake him; for he hath no part nor inheritance with thee. [14:28] At the end of three years thou shalt bring forth all the tithe of thine increase the same year, and shalt lay *it* up within thy gates: [29] And the Levite, (because he hath no part nor inheritance with thee,) and the stranger, and the fatherless, and the widow, which *are* within thy gates, shall come, and shall eat and be satisfied; that the LORD thy God may bless thee in all the work of thine hand which thou doest.

According to verses 22 and 23, the procedure for tithing is the same as in Deuteronomy 12, but with the addition of a frequency. Tithing was to take place **"year by year,"** with a different arrangement for every third year (14:28). As in chapter 12, tithe givers are invited to partake of their tithes. Instructions for those who had to travel a long distance are also covered here. If the distance was too far to carry a large load, the *tither* could sell his tithe, take the money to the place of God's choosing, and buy whatever *he* wanted, to include **"wine or strong drink"** for the celebration before the LORD (14:24-26). *Note that the money itself was not to be tithed.*

The Israelites were reminded not to forsake the **"Levite that is within thy gates"** (14:27). To ensure the Levite is not forsaken, the tithe of every third year was to be stored within each gated community. This was a tithe of produce; **"the tithe of thine increase"** (14:28). On the third year, this tithe of produce was to be set aside exclusively for those Levites, strangers, fatherless, and widows who were living among the people. The final verse deserves special attention, as the blessings of God were contingent upon Israel's faithfulness in providing for these people (14:29).

Deuteronomy 18:1-8: Supporting the Priests and Levites

This passage does not deal with the tithe, but it does detail the support for those serving before the LORD. While the Israelites were responsible to feed the Levites living within each gated community (Deut. 14:27), there would also be Levites who did not live among them. The following section discusses the support for these Levites, as well as the priests who served before the LORD.

Deuteronomy 18:1-8
[18:1] The priests the Levites, *and* all the tribe of Levi, shall have no part nor inheritance with Israel: they shall eat the offerings of the LORD made by fire, and his inheritance. [2] Therefore shall they have no inheritance among their brethren: the LORD *is* their inheritance, as he hath said unto them. [18:3] And this shall be the priest's due from the people, from them that offer a sacrifice, whether *it be* ox or sheep; and they shall give unto the priest the shoulder, and the two cheeks, and the maw. [4] The firstfruit *also* of thy corn, of thy wine, and of thine oil, and the first of the fleece of thy sheep, shalt thou give him. [5] For the LORD thy God hath chosen him out of all thy tribes, to stand to minister in the name of the LORD, him and his sons forever. [6] And if a Levite come from any of thy gates out of all Israel, where he sojourned, and come with all the desire of his mind unto the place which the LORD shall choose; [7] Then he shall minister in the name of the LORD his God, as all his brethren the Levites *do*, which stand there before the LORD. [8] They shall have like portions to eat, beside that which cometh of the sale of his patrimony.

The passage begins by stating that the "**priests the Levites, all the tribe of Levi…, shall eat the offerings of the LORD**" (18:1). Back in Numbers, the offerings had been exclusively reserved for Aaron and his descendants (Num. 18:8-20), while the Levites received the tithes of Israel (Num. 18:21-24). Under this new economy of life in the land, we find that the Levites who ministered in the "**name of the LORD**," in "**the place that the LORD shall choose**" were also to take part in the offerings. God had made adequate provision for His people.

The "**sale of his patrimony**" (18:8) refers to Levites who owned property. In Numbers 35:1-8, God granted forty-eight cities and open land to the Levites. A Levite could own property in one of these cities. The open land, used for farming and livestock, was shared among the priests and Levites living in these cities. Leviticus 25:32-33 describes the redemption rights on a Levite's property, should he decide to sell it.

Deuteronomy 26:1-15: Presenting the Offering

These are the last verses in the Law of Moses referring to the tithe. The first part of the passage details how the firstfruits of the produce were to be presented. The second part covers the third year tithe mentioned in Deuteronomy 14:28-29.

> Deuteronomy 26:1-15
> [26:1] And it shall be, when thou *art* come in unto the land which the LORD thy God giveth thee *for* an inheritance, and possessest it, and dwellest therein; [2] That thou shalt take of the first of all the fruit of the earth, which thou shalt bring of thy land that the LORD thy God giveth thee, and shalt put *it* in a basket, and shalt go unto the place which the LORD thy God shall choose to place his name there. [3] And thou shalt go unto the priest that shall be in those days, and say unto him, I profess this day unto the LORD thy God, that I am

come unto the country which the LORD sware unto our fathers for to give us. [4] And the priest shall take the basket out of thine hand, and set it down before the altar of the LORD thy God. [5] And thou shalt speak and say before the LORD thy God, A Syrian ready to perish *was* my father, and he went down into Egypt, and sojourned there with a few, and became there a nation, great, mighty, and populous: [6] And the Egyptians evil entreated us, and afflicted us, and laid upon us hard bondage: [7] And when we cried unto the LORD God of our fathers, the LORD heard our voice, and looked on our affliction, and our labour, and our oppression: [8] And the LORD brought us forth out of Egypt with a mighty hand, and with an outstretched arm, and with great terribleness, and with signs, and with wonders: [9] And he hath brought us into this place, and hath given us this land, *even* a land that floweth with milk and honey. [10] And now, behold, I have brought the firstfruits of the land, which thou, O LORD, hast given me. And thou shalt set it before the LORD thy God, and worship before the LORD thy God: [11] And thou shalt rejoice in every good *thing* which the LORD thy God hath given unto thee, and unto thine house, thou, and the Levite, and the stranger that *is* among you.

[26:12] When thou hast made an end of tithing all the tithes of thine increase the third year, *which is* the year of tithing, and hast given *it* unto the Levite, the stranger, the fatherless, and the widow, that they may eat within thy gates, and be filled; [13] Then thou shalt say before the LORD thy God, I have brought away the hallowed things out of *mine* house, and also have given them unto the Levite, and unto the stranger, to the fatherless, and to the widow, according to all thy commandments which thou hast commanded me: I have not transgressed thy commandments, neither have I forgotten *them*: [14] I have not eaten thereof in my mourning, neither have I taken away *ought* thereof for *any* unclean *use*, nor given *ought* thereof for the dead: *but* I have hearkened to the voice of the LORD my God, *and* have done according to all that thou hast commanded me. [15] Look down from thy holy habitation, from heaven, and bless thy

people Israel, and the land which thou hast given us, as thou swarest unto our fathers, a land that floweth with milk and honey.

The first verse of this passage reiterates the fact that these instructions were to be followed once the children of Israel were settled in the land (26:1). The actual procedure for presenting the firstfruits of produce to the priest is set forth here. The people were to bring their offerings in baskets. The basket was set before the priest (26:1-2). Upon presenting this offering, the Israelite was to profess to the priest that he had come into the land that the LORD God had promised to the fathers (26:3). The priest would then set the offering before the altar. This being accomplished, the Israelite would continue. The words spoken reflect directly back to Jacob (**"a Syrian ready to perish"**), his going to Egypt **"with a few,"** and becoming a great nation, **"mighty and populous"** (26:5). The **"he"** in verse 5 becomes **"us"** and **"we"** in the verses that follow as the subject is transferred from Jacob to his descendants (26:6-10). It is upon the LORD'S deliverance and bringing them into the land that the presentation of the offering is based (26:8-10).

Here, as in Genesis 28:13-14, we find that Jacob and his descendants are bound into a single unit. In this passage, there is a direct reference to Jacob (26:5), the identifying of the nation with Jacob (26:5-10), and the LORD'S fulfilled promise of bringing them into the land (26:3, 9) in relation to presenting the offering (26:1-3, 5-10). It is as if to say, "God has fulfilled His promise. He has been with us (Num. 9:15-23). He has fed us (Deut. 8:16). He has clothed us (Deut. 8:4). He has given us this land as He had promised." As God's promise was fulfilled through Jacob's descendants (his "seed"), the vow of Jacob (Gen. 28:20-22) was confirmed by his descendants. And the blessings of God are returned as the Israelite is invited to **"rejoice in every good thing which the LORD thy God hath given"** (26:11).

36

The second part of this passage details the third year tithe. The third year was called **"the year of tithing"** (26:12), in which the tithe of produce was stored within each community to be given to **"the Levite, the stranger, the fatherless, and the widow."** It was not taken to the annual feast with the firstfruits and livestock to the place where God's name would dwell. This tithe of produce was to be stored within the local community for those who had no means of provision (26:12; See also 14:28). God's kindness and generosity was to be reflected through the Israelite who gave this tithe.

Here, as in Deuteronomy 14:29, we find that God's blessing upon Israel depended on their faithfulness in giving this particular tithe. It was upon the truthful confirmation of the Israelite that not one part of it was taken for any other purpose, that the blessings of God were attached (26:14-15). Note that God commanded the people to ask for His blessing here. There is a reason for that. God's generosity toward Israel was conditioned upon Israel's ongoing generosity toward those whose lives depended in it (See also Deut. 24:19).

The Law: Final Analysis

Origin of the Biblical Tithe

While we do not know the exact origin of the tithe in ancient cultures, we do know that Abram tithed from the spoils of battle to God's priest. But as there is no additional information regarding this isolated case, we cannot rightly use Abram's tithe as a point of reference for our understanding of the Biblical tithe.

That the Biblical tithe as we know it originated with Jacob's vow is evident in Scripture. At Bethel, the LORD promised to give the land to Jacob and his descendants (Gen. 28:13). Jacob vowed to return a tenth of what God gave him (Gen. 28:20-22). In dealing with vows (Lev. 27), the LORD demanded from Israel exactly what Jacob had vowed (see also Deut. 23:21). Israel received the land, and the LORD claimed the "tithe of the land" (Lev. 27:30). The connection between God's promise and Jacob's vow was confirmed through the Israelite (Jacob's descendant) who, under God's instruction, identified himself with Jacob while presenting the offering (Deut. 26:1-10). The Biblical evidence is clear. The tithe of Israel had its beginning at Bethel with the vow of Jacob.

Tithing Responsibilities and Exemptions

In Genesis 32:28, God gave Jacob a new name: Israel. As we have seen, Israel was to give the tithe of the land, as well as the tithe of the herd and the flock to the LORD in fulfillment of Jacob's vow. And while God does not need a tenth of anything that already belongs to Him, He used that vow in such a way that it became a blessing.

God used the tithe of Israel to feed and clothe His servants working at the tabernacle. He used it to provide for the poor among His people. He multiplied it for an annual feast in which everyone could partake in a celebration before the LORD.

Because Jacob (Israel) made the vow to give the tithe, it was specifically Israel's responsibility to fulfill it (Lev. 27:34). It did not and does not apply to anyone else. Yet even within Israel, there were those who would be exempt from tithing. The LORD's tithe consisted of produce and livestock (Lev. 27:30-33). If one made fishing his profession, he was not required to tithe his fish, nor the money he made selling fish (money was not a tithed item). Carpenters and other craftsmen did not tithe of their handiwork, or of money made from the trade. Widows, orphans, strangers, and others who were poor were not required to tithe. Their sustenance came from sheaves that were left behind during the harvest (Deut. 24:19-22), as well as the tithed produce that was stored every third year and set aside for them.

The requirement to tithe fell upon the eleven tribes who received portions of the land as an inheritance from the LORD. Within each tribe, families owning land and cattle were to give the tithe (Lev. 27:30-34). It also seems reasonable that the priests and Levites who chose to live in their own cities with open land for farming and raising livestock might be required to tithe (Num. 35:2-3).

Widows, Orphans, Strangers

Besides the Levites, the third year tithe was set aside for the widows, orphans and strangers. For widows in those days, not having a husband meant not having the means for support. The same was the case for the fatherless child. Strangers living in the land, not being a part of the local economy, were likewise without means for sustenance. The third year tithe was part of God's plan for supporting these people. The widow and orphan depended on it. That God cares for the stranger also served as a reminder to the Israelites that they too were once strangers in the land of Egypt (Ex. 23:9).

Regarding these people, Scripture abounds with references placing them under the special protection of God. Among the commands that God gave to Moses at Mt. Sinai were these words: "Thou shalt neither vex a stranger, nor oppress him: for ye were strangers in the land of Egypt. Ye shall not afflict any widow, or fatherless child. If thou afflict them in any wise, and they cry at all unto me, I will surely hear their cry; and my wrath shall wax hot, and I will kill you with the sword; and your wives shall be widows, and your children fatherless" (Ex. 22:21-24). Deuteronomy 10:18 tells us that God "administers justice for the fatherless and the widow, and loves the stranger, giving him food and clothing." Psalm 68:5 calls God a "father to the fatherless and defender of widows." In light of these, as well as other passages from Scripture, it is evident that much of Israel's punishment was due to their mistreatment and abuse of the poor among them. God meant what He said. Among those under His special protection are the widow, the orphan, and the stranger. Cross the line with these people and expect to be punished. Israel did, and Israel did not go unpunished.

Did Israel Pay Multiple Tithes?

We have seen that the tithing instructions in Numbers are not the same as those in Deuteronomy. We also learned that the tithing practice as directed in Numbers during Israel's years of wandering would cease once they had settled in the land (Deut. 12:1, 8). Yet there are those who seem to have missed that information, leading to the assumption that a separate, second tithe must be the reason for the difference in instructions. They hold what is called a "second tithe" theory. This is not to be confused with the "king's tithe" of 1st Samuel 8:10-18.

The "second tithe" theory varies, depending on how one views Scripture and its chronology in writing. Liberal scholars, who hold that Deuteronomy was actually written *before* Numbers, see an evolution in tithing. In their view, the tithe began more as a means of sharing. The people at first shared their offerings with the Levites, as we find in Deuteronomy. As time progressed, tithing specifically to the Levites became mandatory, as recorded in Numbers.[7] This view is rejected at once, as it ignores the sequence of events set forth in Scripture, with the years of wandering and the ways of life during the time of the book of Numbers *preceding* Israel's settlement in the land with its different lifestyle, as set forth in Deuteronomy.

Another theory for a second tithe relies on history and tradition. Support for this theory is found in such writings as the *Mishna,*[8] the apocryphal Book of Tobit,[9] as well as the writings of Josephus.[10] While none of these are primary sources, they are ancient. With several ancient testimonies referring to more than one tithe, it is probable that at some point in Israel's history more than one tithe may have been required. However, since these sources were written hundreds of years after the completion of the Old Testament,[11] it is more likely that any additional tithe would find its origin in Israel's later history, after the Babylonian captivity.

---

[7] Merrill C. Tenney, Ed. *The Pictorial Bible Dictionary.* (Zondervan Publishing House, Grand Rapids, MI, 1968), p.857.

[8] *Mishna Yadayim* 4:3. However, this discussion of a seventh year tithe finds no support in Scripture.

[9] *Tobit* 1:6-7.

[10] Whiston, William, Translator: *The Works of Josephus: Antiquities of the Jews,* Book 4, Chapter 8. (Hendrickson Publishers, Inc., Peabody, MA, 1987), p. 119. Hereafter referred to as *Josephus.*

[11] *Mishna:* A first century date is based on the life of Rabbi Eleazar ben Azariah; *Tobit:* 225 – 175 B.C.; *Josephus:* A.D. 37-100.

In the book of Nehemiah, we learn that upon returning to Jerusalem, the people followed the tithing instructions in Numbers,[12] rather than Deuteronomy. Since they had to relearn the Law (Neh. 8), Numbers would have been the first instructions they encountered by order of reading. Once the tithe was established according to Numbers, it is not difficult to see how an additional tithe might be added to that in order to keep the Law according to Deuteronomy as well.

As history attests through writings like the *Mishna* or the canons of Catholicism, it is a known human tendency to misconstrue Scripture and to add to it. Since God in His Law does not mention a separate "second tithe," it is probable that if one was ever required, it occurred during this later period.

A major problem for the "second tithe" theory is that it underestimates the blessings of God. An interesting example comes to us from 2nd Chronicles 31:4-19 (in the next section). During Hezekiah's reforms, tithing was restored. While it is erroneously taught that Israel paid two (or even three) tithes, we can see from this passage that one tithe was more than sufficient to meet the needs of everyone. One tithe from three or four tribes was so large that it took the people four months to bring it all in. Special storage facilities had to be prepared. People had to be sought out in order to receive it. Considering that the instructions in Deuteronomy anticipated tithes from the entirety of Israel, how much more might that have been? Yet there are those who see a need for a second tithe. Should we then consider that the people spent an additional four months transporting the second tithe? Since the very idea is preposterous, we can conclude that the "second tithe" theory is equally absurd.

---

[12] Nehemiah 10:37-38 finds no support in Deuteronomy, but is based on the instructions according to Numbers 18:26-32.

Those who see a need for a second, or even a third tithe, find it difficult to believe that one tithe could sustain all of the priests and Levites for an entire year. Yet we have already seen that once settled in the land, forty-eight cities with land (for cattle or crops) were to be set aside for them (Num. 35:1-8). Also, Levites living among the people were to be regularly supported by those among whom they lived. Every third year, the tithe of produce was to be put into storage for their use, as well as for orphans, widows, and sojourners (Deut. 14:27-29). Scripture does not state that this was an additional tithe, but that this was how the tithe of produce would be used every third year. Regarding the Levites serving with the priests, they were given portions of the regular offerings that supported the priests throughout the year. (Deut. 18:1-8). There was no need for another tithe, nor was one mentioned in Scripture. God never demanded anything more than the tenth that Jacob had committed to Him.

It has also been argued that since Scripture speaks of "tithes" (noting the plurality of the word), that there was more than one tithe and this supports a second or third tithe. But this argument is immediately nullified once we understand that there was a tithe of produce and a tithe of livestock, which can further be broken down into the various kinds of plants and animals that were tithed. Added to that is the fact that there were eleven tribes in Israel with families represented in each tribe. They all tithed. All of these can be taken together in a variety of ways and be called, "tithes," thus accounting for the plurality of the word.

The "second tithe" theory is no more than a theory. As such, it has no Scriptural authority. God specifically instructed the Israelites regarding His tithe. Although the instructions varied according to how it was to be used, only one tithe is mentioned. There were instructions for the wilderness years of wandering, and there were instructions to be followed once Israel had settled in the land. Upon arrival and settlement in the land, the former instructions no longer applied (Deut. 12:8).

Tithes and Offerings

In many churches, congregations are told that if they are not tithing, then anything given as an offering does not count as an offering. Beginning with the assumption that God owns the first ten percent, it is reasoned that anything given less than that is the same as robbing God, and is unacceptable. Once the ten percent is paid (so the argument goes), anything given beyond that is then considered an acceptable offering. Following this line of reasoning, we might ask that if an offering is not acceptable to God, why the church accepts it. But there is no support for this kind of reasoning found in the Bible.

In the Old Testament, the tithe was separate from the various kinds of offerings. There were sin offerings, burnt offerings, peace offerings, and other kinds of offerings, which are detailed in the Book of Leviticus. Each served a different purpose, but they were not a part of the tithe, nor had anything to do with the tithe. One could give any of the various offerings without having given the tithe.

Those who were not landowners could not tithe, since the tithe consisted of produce and livestock. Still, since all have sinned, all must be able to offer a sin offering, and God had made provisions for those without means to make the offering. Leviticus 5:6-13 provides the instruction. If one was not able to offer a lamb, he could offer two turtledoves or two young pigeons (5:7). If that was too much, he could merely bring some fine flour and offer that (5:11). Thus, one could certainly give an offering without having given a tithe.

Tithes and Money

When church leaders mention tithes, they are normally talking about the percentage of money one is expected to give in proportion to his or her income. The Bible, however, does not refer to money as an item to be tithed. Scripture is very specific about what is to be tithed and money is not included. While money was used in *relation to* the tithe, it was never to be used *as* the tithe.

Deuteronomy 14:24-26 explains that the tithe could be exchanged for money if the distance was too far to carry it. Upon arrival at the place God had chosen, the money was used to buy whatever the *tither* desired in order to take part in the celebration before the LORD.

Some argue that money was not used as a tithe in Israel because Israel was an agricultural society. Yet we have just seen that money *was* used in Israel, and how it was to be used in relation to the tithe. The "agricultural society" argument is not based on the facts. Ancient Israel also used money in support of the tabernacle. This, however, was a totally separate offering and had nothing to do with the tithe. Each year on the Day of Atonement, a half shekel was required from every man over twenty years of age. This money, an annual tax, was to be used in the service of the tabernacle (Ex. 30:12-16). If ministers need to collect money for the upkeep of church facilities, this would be a more accurate passage for application. But one must be careful in how to apply the Law to a congregation under Grace.[13] It should be done by example and by way of encouragement, but never by mandate (2nd Cor. 8:8).

---

[13] Salvation according to the New Testament is by the grace of God through the atoning work of Jesus Christ. The Law of the Old Testament does not apply to those covered by God's grace. See Romans 6:14; 7:1-4; Galatians 5:18.

Closing Thoughts

The Biblical tithe was provided by landowners and used for a celebration in which everyone took part, as well as to feed the spiritual leaders and people in need. With such specific instructions regarding the tithe and its use, why are churches being taught differently? Since the Biblical tithe was used to feed the poor, why do churches use it for other things? We have churches taking tithes of money *from* their poor! Since the commandment to tithe fell strictly upon Israel, why do preachers even demand it at all? It is evident, both past and present that one of our tendencies as a fallen race is to teach "for doctrines the commandments of men" (Matthew 15:9).

Chapter 3

The Tithe in the Historical Books

The historical books, Joshua to Nehemiah, focus on events that took place in Israel's history after entering the Promised Land. We get the good, as well as the bad news. In some cases, we are merely provided information with no word as to whether a particular activity was good or bad. In those instances, we may refer back to the Law and see how it measured up to God's instruction.

Of the twelve historical books in the Old Testament, the tithe is specifically mentioned only in 2nd Chronicles and Nehemiah. Yet there are several passages that provide some insight into the practices of Israel, which would include giving tithes and offerings. These deserve our attention. Three of these passages offer a glimpse into Israel's earliest years in the Promised Land, and are found in the books of Joshua, Judges, and 1st Samuel.

Joshua, Judges and 1st Samuel: Reflections of Deuteronomy

In Deuteronomy, the LORD stated that He would cause His name to dwell at a certain place once Israel settled in the land (Deut. 12:5, 11, 14). Joshua 18:1 informs us of such a place.

> **Joshua 18:1**
> **[18:1] And the whole congregation of the children of Israel assembled together at Shiloh, and set up the tabernacle of the congregation there. And the land was subdued before them.**

Here we find that the tabernacle was established at Shiloh. It would remain there throughout the times of the Judges. In Deuteronomy, we also learned that all the tithes, offerings, and sacrifices were to be brought annually to the place where the LORD'S name would dwell (Deut. 14:22-23). There, the people were to eat and rejoice before the LORD (Deut. 14:26).

> **Judges 21:19**
> [21:19] Then they said, Behold, *there is* a feast of the LORD in Shiloh yearly *in a place* which *is* on the north side of Bethel, on the east side of the highway that goeth up from Bethel to Shechem, and on the south of Lebonah.

As the above passages indicate, Shiloh was the place where the LORD caused His name to dwell, as this was where His tabernacle was established (Josh. 18:1). Shiloh was also where the annual feasts took place (Judges 21:19). In the following passage, we have an example of a family eating and sharing portions of their offerings at Shiloh, demonstrating the pattern for tithes and offerings found in Deuteronomy.

> **1st Samuel 1:1-5**
> [1:1] Now there was a certain man of Ramathaimzophim, of mount Ephraim, and his name *was* Elkanah, the son of Jeroham, the son of Elihu, the son of Tohu, the son of Zuph, an Ephrathite: [2] And he had two wives; the name of the one *was* Hannah, and the name of the other Peninnah: and Peninnah had children, but Hannah had no children. [3] And this man went up out of his city yearly to worship and to sacrifice unto the LORD of hosts in Shiloh. And the two sons of Eli, Hophni and Phinehas, the priests of the LORD, *were* there. [4] And when the time was that Elkanah offered, he gave to Peninnah his wife, and to all her sons and her daughters, portions: [5] But unto Hannah he gave a worthy portion; for he loved Hannah: but the LORD had shut up her womb.

According to this passage, Elkanah took his family **"yearly to worship and sacrifice unto the LORD of hosts in Shiloh"** (1:3). When Elkanah **"offered"** his sacrifice, he gave every member of his family **"portions"** (1:4-5). The Scriptural evidence demonstrates that in her earliest years in the Promised Land, Israel followed the procedures in Deuteronomy for tithes and offerings. There is no indication that the instructions in the Book of Numbers were followed once the children of Israel were established in the land.

2nd Chronicles 31:4-19: Abundance

The first specific reference to the tithe in the historical books is found in 2nd Chronicles 31 as a part of King Hezekiah's reforms. Hezekiah was the son of King Ahaz, whose reign is described in 2nd Chronicles 28. Ahaz caused Judah to turn from God to worship idols. He removed items from the temple of God and destroyed them. Ahaz shut down the temple and built altars for idol worship all over Jerusalem (28:24).

Unlike his father Ahaz, Hezekiah worshiped the LORD. When he became king, Hezekiah began to restore Judah to the worship of God. He reopened the temple (29:3), restored worship there (29:20-36), and destroyed the idols and their altars (31:1). Along with King Hezekiah's reforms came the restoration of the tithes and firstfruits for the support of the priests and Levites.

> 2nd Chronicles 31:4-19
> [31:4] Moreover he commanded the people that dwelt in Jerusalem to give the portion of the priests and the Levites, that they might be encouraged in the law of the LORD. [5] And as soon as the commandment came abroad, the children of Israel brought in abundance the firstfruits of corn, wine, and oil, and honey, and of all the increase of the field; and the tithe of all *things* brought they in abundantly. [6] And

49

concerning the children of Israel and Judah, that dwelt in the cities of Judah, they also brought in the tithe of oxen and sheep, and the tithe of holy things which were consecrated unto the LORD their God, and laid *them* by heaps. [7] In the third month they began to lay the foundation of the heaps, and finished *them* in the seventh month.

[31:8] And when Hezekiah and the princes came and saw the heaps, they blessed the LORD, and his people Israel. [9] Then Hezekiah questioned with the priests and the Levites concerning the heaps. [10] And Azariah the chief priest of the house of Zadok answered him, and said, Since *the people* began to bring the offerings into the house of the LORD, we have had enough to eat, and have left plenty: for the LORD hath blessed his people; and that which is left *is* this great store.

[31:11] Then Hezekiah commanded to prepare chambers in the house of the LORD; and they prepared *them*, [12] And brought in the offerings and the tithes and the dedicated *things* faithfully: over which Cononiah the Levite *was* ruler, and Shimei his brother *was* the next. [13] And Jehiel, and Azaziah, and Nahath, and Asahel, and Jerimoth, and Jozabad, and Eliel, and Ismachiah, and Mahath, and Benaiah, *were* overseers under the hand of Cononiah and Shimei his brother, at the commandment of Hezekiah the king, and Azariah the ruler of the house of God. [14] And Kore the son of Imnah the Levite, the porter toward the east, *was* over the freewill offerings of God, to distribute the oblations of the LORD, and the most holy things. [15] And next him *were* Eden, and Miniamin, and Jeshua, and Shemaiah, Amariah, and Shecaniah, in the cities of the priests, in *their* set office, to give to their brethren by courses, as well to the great as to the small: [16] Beside their genealogy of males, from three years old and upward, *even* unto every one that entereth into the house of the LORD, his daily portion for their service in their charges according to their courses; [17] Both to the genealogy of the priests by the house of their fathers, and the Levites from twenty years old and upward, in their charges by their courses; [18] And to the genealogy of all their little ones, their wives, and their sons, and their daughters, through all the congregation: for in their set office they sanctified themselves in holiness: [19] Also of the sons of Aaron the priests, *which were* in the fields of the suburbs of their cities, in every several city, the men that were expressed by name, to give portions to all the males among the priests, and to all that were reckoned by genealogies among the Levites.

This is the one and only detailed account in Scripture of the people bringing in their firstfruits and tithes. It is apparent that after the initial feast (31:10), the remaining quantity was more than sufficient to sustain the priests and Levites serving at the temple. The abundance was so massive that it took four months for the people to transport it (31:7). Additional storage facilities had to be built (31:11). The blessing was such that even priests living in the Levitical cities with their own farmland were sought out to receive portions (31:19). This one account of a single tithe is a testimony to the blessings of God toward His people when they acknowledge Him. Keep in mind that the kingdom was divided at this time, and this offering came from only three or four of the twelve tribes (2nd Chron. 31:1).

Nehemiah: Back to the Book of Numbers

The focus of the book of Nehemiah is the return to Jerusalem that took place under Persian rule after the Babylonian captivity. Nehemiah led in rebuilding the wall of Jerusalem. During this time, he confronted problems with the people who lived in the land, as well as the Jews who were influenced by them. It is in this context and struggle that the tithe is mentioned in several places throughout the book.

Nehemiah 10:37-39
[10:37] And *that* we should bring the firstfruits of our dough, and our offerings, and the fruit of all manner of

trees, of wine and of oil, unto the priests, to the chambers of the house of our God; and the tithes of our ground unto the Levites, that the same Levites might have the tithes in all the cities of our tillage. [38] And the priest the son of Aaron shall be with the Levites, when the Levites take tithes: and the Levites shall bring up the tithe of the tithes unto the house of our God, to the chambers, into the treasure house. [39] For the children of Israel and the children of Levi shall bring the offering of the corn, of the new wine, and the oil, unto the chambers, where *are* the vessels of the sanctuary, and the priests that minister, and the porters, and the singers: and we will not forsake the house of our God.

From this passage, it is evident that Nehemiah and those with him were following the tithing procedures from the book of Numbers rather than Deuteronomy. In Numbers, we learned that Aaron and his sons (the priests) received the firstfruits, offerings, and the best of the wine and oil (Num. 18:8-19), while the Levites received the tithe of the people (Num. 18:24). Here in Nehemiah, the procedure is the same (10:37). In the book of Numbers, the Levites were to offer a tenth of the tithe to Aaron the priest (Num. 18:28). This also occurs here: **"the Levites shall bring up the tithe of the tithes"** (10:38).

Nehemiah's return to the book of Numbers for tithing instructions creates a problem, as those directions were specific to Israel's forty years of wandering before entering the Promised Land. The book of Deuteronomy states that those procedures would no longer apply once Israel had settled in the land (Deut. 12:1, 8).

Yet when we consider the seventy year break from their continuity of practice, it is understandable that the Jews would have to relearn certain ordinances. This relearning took place upon the public reading of the Law in the eighth chapter of Nehemiah. In that chapter we find the Jews learning again how to keep the feast of tabernacles (Neh. 8:14-17). The instruction they followed for that is found in the book of Leviticus (Lev. 23:39-44).

Regarding the tithe, by order of reading, Numbers would have been the first instruction the people heard. That they immediately practiced tithing according to the book of Numbers demonstrates their eagerness to get right with God, but it is evident throughout Nehemiah that they never followed any of the tithing procedures set forth in Deuteronomy. Every instance of tithing in Nehemiah can only be traced to the book of Numbers. As there is no explanation for this discrepancy, it is likely that the Jewish leaders, in their haste to return to the proper practice of the Law of Moses, emphasized the wrong set of instructions.

Nehemiah 12:44-47

[12:44] And at that time were some appointed over the chambers for the treasures, for the offerings, for the firstfruits, and for the tithes, to gather into them out of the fields of the cities the portions of the law for the priests and Levites: for Judah rejoiced for the priests and for the Levites that waited. [45] And both the singers and the porters kept the ward of their God, and the ward of the purification, according to the commandment of David, *and* of Solomon his son. [46] For in the days of David and Asaph of old *there were* chief of the singers, and songs of praise and thanksgiving unto God. [47] And all Israel in the days of Zerubbabel, and in the days of Nehemiah, gave the portions of the singers and the porters, every day his portion: and they sanctified *holy things* unto the Levites; and the Levites sanctified *them* unto the children of Aaron.

This is Nehemiah's system of accountability for the tithes and offerings. In verse 44, we learn that there were men appointed to oversee their gathering and storage. As in Nehemiah 10:39, we read that the singers and porters were given a portion (12:47). Thus far, the third year tithe has not been mentioned, nor has there been any word of support for the widow, orphan or stranger in relation to the tithe (Deut. 14:28-29). Again, the last part of verse 47 reflects the tithing instructions from the book of Numbers (Num. 18:26).

Nehemiah 13:4-12

[13:4] And before this, Eliashib the priest, who was set over the rooms of the house of our God, who *was* related to Tobiah, [5] (and he had prepared for himself a large room and there before they were giving the food offering, the frankincense, and the vessels, and the tithes of the grain, the new wine, and the oil, which was commanded *to be given* to the Levites, and the singers, and the gatekeepers, and the offerings of the priests). [6] But in all this *time* I was not at Jerusalem. For in the thirty second year of Artaxerxes the king of Babylon, I came to the king. And after some days I asked leave from the king. [7] And I came to Jerusalem, and understood the evil which Eliashib did for Tobiah, in preparing a room for him in the courts of the house of God. [8] And it grieved me very much. And I threw all the household stuff of Tobiah out of the room.
[13:9] Then I commanded, and they purified the rooms. And I returned there the vessels of the house of God, with the food offering and the frankincense. [10] And I was aware that the portions of the Levites had not been given, for the Levites and the singers who did the work had each one fled to his field. [11] Then I contended with the rulers, and said, Why is the house of God forsaken? And I gathered them and set them in their place. [12] Then all Judah brought the tithe of the grain, and the new wine, and the oil, into the treasuries.

This particular situation involved two individuals, Eliashib and Tobiah. While Nehemiah was away to see the king, Eliashib had cleaned out one of the storage rooms at the temple so that Tobiah could reside there (13:4-7). Upon his return, Nehemiah threw Tobiah out, purified the rooms, and returned the items that belonged in them (13:8-9).

By virtue of the fact that the Levites and singers had returned to their fields to work for their food (13:10), and Nehemiah's observation that the house of God had been **"forsaken"** (13:11), it is evident that the rooms had not been used for their intended purpose for a considerable amount of time. After Nehemiah had contended with the rulers, the tithe was once again restored (13:12).

The Historical Books: Final Analysis

Reflections of Deuteronomy

The books of Joshua, Judges, and 1st Samuel, provide glimpses into the earliest activities of Israel in the Promised Land. The tabernacle was established at Shiloh, where the people would offer their tithes, sacrifices and offerings, and also partake of their offerings as they shared their blessings among family and friends (1st Sam. 1:4). These practices reflect the instructions found in Deuteronomy. There is nothing in these books comparable to the tithing procedures from the Book of Numbers.

The Blessing of God

2nd Chronicles 31:4-19 gives a detailed account of a tithe collected from three or four tribes out of the divided kingdom, as part of Hezekiah's reforms.[14] The abundance was such that it took the people four months to bring it all in, and after the feast the remainder of the offering was so great that there was no room to store it all (31:6-10). Special facilities were constructed. Priests and Levites were sought throughout the land out to receive portions. God had blessed His people.

Nehemiah

While the other historical books reflect Deuteronomy in regard to tithing procedures, Nehemiah's instructions follow the book of Numbers. There is no indication of any influence from Deuteronomy in Nehemiah about the use of the tithe. Priests and Levites received tithes, but widows, orphans, and strangers are not mentioned; nor is there any mention of the third year tithe.

---

[14] 2nd Chronides 31:1 mentions Benjamin, Judah, Ephraim and Manasseh.

This makes sense if Nehemiah was following the book of Numbers alone for direction in the practice of tithes and offerings. Numbers would have been the first tithing instructions confronted in the Law by order of reading (Neh. 8), and it is reasonable that Nehemiah and those with him would have begun following those instructions upon learning them.

While the book of Nehemiah provides his personal account of what took place during a time in Israel's post-exilic history, it contains no direct word from God indicating whether the events recorded were right or wrong. One must consult the Law (Exodus 20 through Deuteronomy) and the Prophets (Malachi in particular[15]) in order to gain a more accurate understanding in that regard. As Nehemiah's use of the tithe leads to questions and controversy rather than a solid foundation in what should be supporting documentation, the book of Nehemiah cannot rightly be used as an authoritative source in regard to tithes and offerings.

---

[15] The circumstances addressed by Malachi parallel the events described in Ezra and Nehemiah, and most scholars date the writing of Malachi to the same time frame. See also Walvoord and Zuck, p. 1573, and *The Believer's Study Bible*, p. 1303. Among the items addressed by Malachi is the improper practice of tithing.

Chapter 4

The Prophets and the Tithe: Robbing God

While the word, "tithe," is found only in Amos and Malachi, its role in the prophets is far greater than many people recognize. In the prophets we read that Israel and Judah stood guilty before God. Among the charges listed against them was the neglect and abuse of their poor. And while the tithe itself is not mentioned, we are directed to those whose lives depended on it for their livelihood. The widow, the fatherless, and the stranger are the subject matter and serve as a reminder. Israel lost her blessing for the simple reason that she no longer met the condition God had placed upon receiving it (Deut. 14:28-29). Israel would also suffer God's wrath for the neglect and abuse of the very people under God's special protection (Ex. 22:21-24). By examining the references to these people as they are found throughout the prophetic books, perhaps we might gain a better understanding of the meaning of Scripture when it comes to "robbing God."

The Prophets: Widows, Orphans and Strangers

Along with the Levites, Deuteronomy tells us that the widow, the fatherless, and the stranger were recipients of the third year tithe. As we have already seen, these people were under God's special protection. While the following passages do not specifically mention the tithe, they provide some insight regarding the people who were to be supported by it, and shed light on at least one reason Israel suffered the wrath of God.

Isaiah 1:14-23

[1:14] Your new moons and your appointed feasts my soul hateth: they are a trouble unto me; I am weary to bear *them*. [15] And when ye spread forth your hands, I will hide mine eyes from you: yea, when ye make many prayers, I will not hear: your hands are full of blood. [16] Wash you, make you clean; put away the evil of your doings from before mine eyes; cease to do evil; [17] **Learn to do well; seek judgment, relieve the oppressed, judge the fatherless, plead for the widow.**
[1:18] Come now, and let us reason together, saith the LORD: though your sins be as scarlet, they shall be as white as snow; though they be red like crimson, they shall be as wool. [19] If ye be willing and obedient, ye shall eat the good of the land: [20] But if ye refuse and rebel, ye shall be devoured with the sword: for the mouth of the LORD hath spoken *it*.
[1:21] How is the faithful city become an harlot! It was full of judgment; righteousness lodged in it; but now murderers. [22] Thy silver is become dross, thy wine mixed with water: [23] **Thy princes *are* rebellious, and companions of thieves: every one loveth gifts, and followeth after rewards: they judge not the fatherless; neither doth the cause of the widow come unto them.**

Isaiah 10:1-2

[10:1] Woe unto them that decree unrighteous decrees, and that write grievousness *which* they have prescribed; [2] **To turn aside the needy from judgment, and to take away the right from the poor of my people, that widows may be their prey, and *that* they may rob the fatherless!**

Jeremiah 5:26-29

[5:26] For among my people are found wicked *men:* they lay wait, as he that setteth snares; they set a trap, they catch men. [27] As a cage is full of birds, so *are* their houses full of deceit: therefore they are become great, and waxen rich. [28] They are waxen fat, they shine: yea, they overpass the deeds of the wicked: **they judge not the cause, the cause of the fatherless, yet they prosper; and the right of the needy do they not** judge. [29] Shall I not visit for these *things?* saith the LORD: shall not my soul be avenged on such a nation as this?

Jeremiah 7:6-7
[7:6] *If* ye oppress not the stranger, the fatherless, and the widow, and shed not innocent blood in this place, neither walk after other gods to your hurt: [7] Then will I cause you to dwell in this place, in the land that I gave to your fathers, forever and ever.

Jeremiah 22:1-5
[22:1] Thus saith the LORD; Go down to the house of the king of Judah, and speak there this word, [2] And say, Hear the word of the LORD, O king of Judah, that sittest upon the throne of David, thou, and thy servants, and thy people that enter in by these gates:
[22:3] Thus saith the LORD; Execute ye judgment and righteousness, and deliver the spoiled out of the hand of the oppressor: and do no wrong, **do no violence to the stranger, the fatherless, nor the widow, neither shed innocent blood in this place.** [4] For if ye do this thing indeed, then shall there enter in by the gates of this house kings sitting upon the throne of David, riding in chariots and on horses, he, and his servants, and his people. [5] But **if ye will not hear these words, I swear by myself, saith the LORD, that this house shall become a desolation.**

Ezekiel 22:6-7
[22:6] Behold, the princes of Israel, every one were in thee to their power to shed blood. [7] In thee have they set light by father and mother: **in the midst of thee have they dealt by oppression with the stranger: in thee have they vexed the fatherless and the widow.**

Ezekiel 22:28-29
[22:28] And her prophets have daubed them with untempered *mortar,* seeing vanity, and divining lies unto them, saying, Thus saith the Lord GOD, when the LORD hath not spoken.

[29] The people of the land have used oppression, and exercised robbery, **and have vexed the poor and needy: yea, they have oppressed the stranger wrongfully.**

Zechariah 7:8-12

[7:8] And the word of the LORD came unto Zechariah, saying, [9] Thus speaketh the LORD of hosts, saying, Execute true judgment, and shew mercy and compassions every man to his brother: [10] And **oppress not the widow, nor the fatherless, the stranger, nor the poor;** and let none of you imagine evil against his brother in your heart.
[7:11] But they refused to hearken, and pulled away the shoulder, and stopped their ears, that they should not hear. [12] Yea, they made their hearts *as* an adamant stone, lest they should hear the law, and the words which the LORD of hosts hath sent in his spirit by the former prophets: therefore came a great wrath from the LORD of hosts.

According to these passages in the prophetic books, the very people who were to be fed from Israel's tithe were abused and neglected. The call of God in these passages is not only to stop the abuse, but to be proactive toward justice and mercy for these people. Remember that the condition of God's blessing was contingent upon Israel's care for these people (Deut. 14:29). He had placed His special protection on them, and His warning serves as a reminder. Because Israel did not heed God's words, Israel lost her blessing and suffered God's wrath. God does not change.

Amos 4:4-5

Amos is the first prophet who specifically mentions the tithe, and it is the third year tithe that is addressed.

> **Amos 4:4-5**
> **[4:4] Come to Bethel, and transgress; at Gilgal multiply transgression; and bring your sacrifices every morning, *and* your tithes after three years: [5] And offer a sacrifice of thanksgiving with leaven, and proclaim *and* publish the free offerings: for this liketh you, O ye children of Israel, saith the Lord GOD.**

The Hebrew word translated to mean *years* in this passage is also the normal Hebrew word for *days*. For this reason, some modern translators have chosen to use the word, *days,* rather than *years* in this passage.[16] However, there are at least two considerations that must be addressed to ensure a proper translation. The first is that there are other Old Testament passages that use this same Hebrew word to mean *year,* which all Hebrew scholars readily recognize.[17] The second is the context that verifies the usage of the word. There is no Scriptural precedent in reference to the tithe where three *days* carries any significant meaning. The third *year* tithe, however, is Biblical. The context of Amos is more easily understood when confirmed by similar references, and the tithe "after three *years*" makes the most sense.

Amos reveals the neglect and abuse of the poor by Israel's wealthy. Again, we are told in Deuteronomy that God's blessings upon Israel depended on Israel's care for

---

[16] Versions include the English Standard Version, the New American Standard Version, as well as the New King James, among others. The NIV leaves it as *three years*, but includes a footnote offering the alternative translation.

[17] Lev. 25:29 and 1st Sam. 27:7 are two examples. See also Wilson, William, *Wilson's Old Testament Word Studies*, p. 493 (Peabody MA: Hendrickson Publishers) and Harris, Archer and Waltke, *Theological Wordbook of the Old Testament*, Vol. 1, p. 370 (Chicago: Moody Press, 1980).

the poor who were among them (Deut. 14:29). While the bulk of Amos foretells the impending wrath to come, one primary reason for condemnation is repeated throughout his prophecy.

Amos 2:6-8

[2:6] Thus saith the LORD; For three transgressions of Israel, and for four, I will not turn away *the punishment* thereof; because **they sold the righteous for silver, and the poor for a pair of shoes; [7] that pant after the dust of the earth on the head of the poor, and turn aside the way of the meek**: and a man and his father will go in unto the *same* maid, to profane my holy name: [8] And they lay *themselves* down upon clothes laid to pledge by every altar, and they drink the wine of the condemned *in* the house of their god.

Amos 3:9-10

[3:9] Publish in the palaces at Ashdod, and in the palaces in the land of Egypt, and say, Assemble yourselves upon the mountains of Samaria, and behold the great tumults in the midst thereof, **and the oppressed in the midst thereof**. [10] For they know not to do right, saith the LORD, who store up violence and robbery in their palaces.

Amos 4:1

[4:1] Hear this word, ye cows of Bashan, that *are* in the mountain of Samaria, **which oppress the poor, which crush the needy**, which say to their masters, Bring, and let us drink.

Amos 5:11-12

[5:11] **Forasmuch therefore as your treading *is* upon the poor,** and ye take from him burdens of wheat: ye have built houses of hewn stone, but ye shall not dwell in them; ye have planted pleasant vineyards, but ye shall not drink wine of them. [12] For I know your manifold transgressions and your mighty sins: they afflict the just, they take a bribe, and **they turn aside the poor** in the gate *from their right*.

Amos 8:4-7

[8:4] Hear this, **O ye that swallow up the needy, even to make the poor of the land to fail,** [5] Saying, When will the new moon be gone, that we may sell corn? And the Sabbath, that we may set forth wheat, making the ephah small, and the shekel great, and falsifying the balances by deceit? [6] **That we may buy the poor for silver, and the needy for a pair of shoes;** *yea,* and sell the refuse of the wheat? [7] The LORD hath sworn by the excellency of Jacob, Surely I will never forget any of their works.

These passages in Amos reveal the fact that the poor were severely mistreated. Regarding the tithe for the poor, it appears that every three years it was carried to Gilgal and Bethel rather than being stored within each community to feed those without means. God had warned Israel beforehand of the consequences for mistreating the poor among them.

Exodus 22:22-27

[22:22] Ye shall not afflict any widow, or fatherless child. [23] If thou afflict them in any wise, and they cry at all unto me, I will surely hear their cry; [24] and my wrath shall wax hot, and I will kill you with the sword; and your wives shall be widows, and your children fatherless.

[22:25] If thou lend money to *any of* my people *that is* poor by thee, thou shalt not be to him as an usurer, neither shalt thou lay upon him usury.

[22:26] If thou at all take thy neighbour's raiment to pledge, thou shalt deliver it unto him by that the sun goeth down: [27] For that *is* his covering only, it *is* his raiment for his skin: wherein shall he sleep? And it shall come to pass, when he crieth unto me, that I will hear; for I *am* gracious.

Malachi 3:1-11

The third chapter of Malachi is frequently quoted by preachers when teaching congregations about tithing. Beginning with verse eight, people are taught that by not tithing to the church, they are robbing God. But when we begin that far into the chapter, we miss a vital element necessary for a correct understanding of the passage. The verses immediately preceding verse eight are essential for an accurate interpretation within its proper context.

Malachi 3:1-11
[3:1] Behold, I will send my messenger, and he shall prepare the way before me: and the Lord, whom ye seek, shall suddenly come to his temple, even the messenger of the covenant, whom ye delight in: behold, he shall come, saith the LORD of hosts.
[3:2] But who may abide the day of his coming? And who shall stand when he appeareth? for he *is* like a refiner's fire, and like fullers' soap: [3] And he shall sit *as* a refiner and purifier of silver: and he shall purify the sons of Levi, and purge them as gold and silver, that they may offer unto the LORD an offering in righteousness.
[3:4] Then shall the offering of Judah and Jerusalem be pleasant unto the LORD, as in the days of old, and as in former years. [5] And I will come near to you to judgment; and I will be a swift witness against the sorcerers, and against the adulterers, and against false swearers, and against those that oppress the hireling in *his* wages, the widow, and the fatherless, and that turn aside the stranger *from his right,* and fear not me, saith the LORD of hosts.
[3:6] For I *am* the LORD, I change not; therefore ye sons of Jacob are not consumed.
[3:7] Even from the days of your fathers ye are gone away from mine ordinances, and have not kept *them.* Return unto me, and I will return unto you, saith the LORD of hosts. But ye said, wherein shall we return? [8] Will a man rob God? Yet ye have robbed me. But ye say, Wherein have we robbed thee? In tithes and offerings. [9] Ye *are* cursed with a curse:

for ye have robbed me, *even* this whole nation. [10] Bring ye all the tithes into the storehouse, that there may be meat in mine house, and prove me now herewith, saith the LORD of hosts, if I will not open you the windows of heaven, and pour you out a blessing, that *there shall* not *be room* enough *to receive it* [11] And I will rebuke the devourer for your sakes, and he shall not destroy the fruits of your ground; neither shall your vine cast her fruit before the time in the field, saith the LORD of hosts.

Here we are informed that upon the coming of the Lord, He will **"purify the sons of Levi so that they may offer unto the LORD an offering in righteousness"** (3:3). He **"will be a swift witness... against those who oppress the hireling in his wages, the widow, the fatherless and that turn aside the stranger"** (3:5). Among the other charges, this passage refers to the oppression of people who were to find their sustenance in the third year tithe (Deut. 14:28), and were under God's special protection (Ex. 22:21-23).

It is upon the foundation of the first five verses that the LORD reminds His people that He does not change (3:6), and tells them that they had departed from His ordinances and needed to return to Him (3:7). The climax is the rhetorical questioning that leads into their condemnation of robbing God (3:7-9). Because Malachi specifically directs our attention to the recipients of the third year tithe in beginning the accusation, it stands to reason that there was a serious lack in setting aside food for the hungry. **"Storehouse"** tithing (3:10) here refers to food (meat). We do not rob God by depriving a church denomination of ten percent of our monetary incomes. We rob God when we refuse to help the needy that He places along our paths.

The Prophets and the Tithe:
Final Analysis

The prophets called for Israel to return to God and to return to His ways. One of His ways as expressed through His people was to provide sustenance for the poor among them. Yet as they departed from God, they departed from His ways, and the most vulnerable among them were neglected and abused as a result. Condemnation for Israel came in two forms. One was the loss of God's blessing:

Amos 4:7-8

[4:7] **And also I have withholden the rain from you**, when *there were* yet three months to the harvest: and I caused it to rain upon one city, and caused it not to rain upon another city: one piece was rained upon, and the piece whereupon it rained not withered. [8] So two *or* three cities wandered unto one city, to drink water; but they were not satisfied: **yet have ye not returned unto me, saith the LORD.**

The other form of condemnation was that Israel would be on the receiving end of the wrath of God.

Exodus 22:22

[22:22] Ye shall not afflict any widow, or fatherless child. [23] If thou afflict them in any wise, and they cry at all unto me, I will surely hear their cry; [24] **And my wrath shall wax hot, and I will kill you with the sword; and your wives shall be widows, and your children fatherless.**

Amos 6:14

[6:14] But, behold, **I will raise up against you a nation**, O house of Israel, saith the LORD the God of hosts; **and they shall afflict you** from the entering in of Hemath unto the river of the wilderness.

The rest is history.

Chapter 5

The Tithe in the New Testament

In the New Testament, the tithe appears in Matthew, Luke and Hebrews. The first occurrence is shared by both Matthew and Luke, in referring to the same event. In Matthew 23:23 and Luke 11:42, Jesus mentions the tithe while dealing out the "woes" to the scribes and Pharisees. The tithe is mentioned again in Luke 18:12, in Christ's analogy of the prayers offered in the temple by the Pharisee and the tax collector. In the seventh chapter of the Book of Hebrews, the tithe of Abraham is used to demonstrate the superiority of Christ over the Levitical priesthood of the Mosaic covenant.

Acts 15:22-30 is also included in this section, because it is the first council of the church. The problem addressed at that council was whether or not Gentile (non-Jewish) believers were required to keep the Law of Moses. While the council concluded that Gentile believers should not be compelled to keep the Law, it did advise that they maintain several "necessary things" (Acts 15:28). The tithe is not found among them.

Matthew 23:23 and Luke 11:42

The following two passages are often used to demonstrate the attitude of Christ toward the tithe. It is pointed out that Jesus affirmed the practice of tithing here.[18] While the main thrust of the message is that the Pharisees had ignored the weightier matters of the Law, they were "not to leave the other undone." This "other"

---

[18]   *Believer's Study Bible*, Luke 11:42 note, p. 1461.

would be the tithe. It is concluded that Jesus still expects the tithe to be paid.

> **Matthew 23:23**
> [23:23] Woe unto you, scribes and Pharisees, hypocrites! For ye pay tithe of mint and anise and cummin, and have omitted the weightier *matters* of the law, judgment, mercy, and faith: these ought ye to have done, and not to leave the other undone.

> **Luke 11:42**
> [11:42] But woe unto you, Pharisees! For ye tithe mint and rue and all manner of herbs, and pass over judgment and the love of God: these ought ye to have done, and not to leave the other undone.

While these verses seem to provide a powerful argument for tithing, their context has Jesus addressing people who are under the Law. With that in mind, in another place we find Jesus instructing an individual to show himself to the priest and to leave an offering according to the Law of Moses (Matthew 8:4). Today we don't practice the Law of Moses. We don't show ourselves to priests, and we are not required to tithe. There is no support in this passage for requiring tithes on this side of the cross.

Luke 18:10-14

In these verses out of Luke's gospel, Jesus refers to the tithe in the parable of the publican and the Pharisee.

> **Luke 18:10-14**
> [18:10] Two men went up into the temple to pray; the one a Pharisee, and the other a publican. [11] The Pharisee stood and prayed thus with himself, God, I thank thee, that I am not as other men *are*, extortioners, unjust, adulterers, or even as this publican. [12] I fast twice in the week, I give tithes of all that I possess. [13] And the publican, standing afar off,

would not lift up so much as *his* eyes unto heaven, but smote upon his breast, saying, God be merciful to me a sinner. [14] I tell you, this man went down to his house justified *rather* than the other: for every one that exalteth himself shall be abased; and he that humbleth himself shall be exalted.

The Pharisee mentioned the fact that he gave tithes of all he possessed (18:12). Giving tithes in this example is nothing more than an occasion for boasting, or exalting one's self. There is no basis for argument here supporting a modern requirement to tithe.

Hebrews 7:1-10

Hebrews 7 has the most detailed treatment of the tithe found in the New Testament. But rather than an encouragement to continue the Old Testament practice, the tithe in this context is used to demonstrate the superiority of Melchizedec (and ultimately, Christ) over the Levitical priesthood.

Hebrews 7:1-10
[7:1] For this Melchisedec, king of Salem, priest of the most high God, who met Abraham returning from the slaughter of the kings, and blessed him; [2] To whom also Abraham gave a tenth part of all; first being by interpretation King of righteousness, and after that also King of Salem, which is, King of peace; [3] Without father, without mother, without descent, having neither beginning of days, nor end of life; but made like unto the Son of God; abideth a priest continually.
[7:4] Now consider how great this man *was,* unto whom even the patriarch Abraham gave the tenth of the spoils. [5] And verily they that are of the sons of Levi, who receive the office of the priesthood, have a commandment to take tithes of the people according to the law, that is, of their brethren, though they come out of the loins of Abraham: [6] But he whose descent is not counted from them received tithes of Abraham, and blessed him that had the promises. [7] And

> without all contradiction the less is blessed of the better. [8] And here men that die receive tithes; but there he *receiveth them,* of whom it is witnessed that he liveth. [9] And as I may so say, Levi also, who receiveth tithes, payed tithes in Abraham. [10] For he was yet in the loins of his father, when Melchisedec met him.

While these verses could possibly be skewed to make an argument in favor of tithing, that is not the intent of the passage. Here the writer of Hebrews demonstrates the superiority of Melchizedec over the Levitical priesthood. Two arguments are used in this passage to make the point. One is the blessing. Melchizedec blessed Abraham, and the point is made that the lesser is blessed by the greater (7:1, 7). The other argument is the tithe. Abraham gave a tenth of the spoils to Melchizedec (7:2, 4-6). Melchizedec's superiority is shown in that the Levites, while yet in the loins of Abraham, paid tithes to him (7:9-10). In demonstrating the superiority of Melchizedec, the writer has demonstrated the superiority of Christ. The priesthood of Jesus, after the order of Melchizedec, is of a higher order than the Levitical priesthood.[19]

Hebrews 5:5-6

[5:5] So also Christ glorified not himself to be made an high priest; but he that said unto him, Thou art my Son, today have I begotten thee. [6] As he saith also in another *place,* Thou *art* a priest for ever after the order of Melchisedec.

Acts 15:22-30

Acts 15 does not mention the tithe, and this passage is included for precisely that reason. Acts 15 contains what has come to be called the Jerusalem Council. The apostles and elders in Jerusalem assembled to consider

---

[19] See also MacDonald, William, *The Believer's Bible Commentary*, p. 52 (Nashville, Thomas Nelson Publishers, 1995)

what to do about the Gentiles who had received the gospel. At issue was whether or not they should be made subject to the Law of Moses.

> **Acts 15:22-30**
> [15:22] Then pleased it the apostles and elders, with the whole church, to send chosen men of their own company to Antioch with Paul and Barnabas; *namely,* Judas surnamed Barsabas, and Silas, chief men among the brethren: [23] And they wrote *letters* by them after this manner; The apostles and elders and brethren *send* greeting unto the brethren which are of the Gentiles in Antioch and Syria and Cilicia: [24] Forasmuch as we have heard, that certain which went out from us have troubled you with words, subverting your souls, saying, *Ye must* be circumcised, and keep the law: to whom we gave no *such* commandment: [25] It seemed good unto us, being assembled with one accord, to send chosen men unto you with our beloved Barnabas and Paul, [26] Men that have hazarded their lives for the name of our Lord Jesus Christ. [27] We have sent therefore Judas and Silas, who shall also tell *you* the same things by mouth. [28] For it seemed good to the Holy Ghost, and to us, to lay upon you no greater burden than these necessary things; [29] That ye abstain from meats offered to idols, and from blood, and from things strangled, and from fornication: from which if ye keep yourselves, ye shall do well. Fare ye well.

If ever there was an opportunity to introduce the tithe to the church, this would have been it. The Gentile believers were newcomers to the grace of God, and it would seem that if tithing existed at all in the Jerusalem church, it would be among the items listed for the Gentiles to practice as well. The fact that it is not speaks volumes.

The Tithe in the New Testament: Final Analysis

No Command for Christians to Tithe

In every New Testament passage where the tithe is found, there is not one command requiring it of Christians. When it is mentioned, the context is either the Law, which was still in effect during Jesus' earthly ministry, or in the case of the book of Hebrews, it is used to demonstrate the superiority of Christ over the Levitical priesthood. If the tithe were to be carried over from the Old Testament to be practiced in the church, it would seem that there would be some passage to that effect. There are none. Again, if tithing was an expected practice in the early church, it would seem that the apostles and elders would have mentioned that to the Gentile believers in Acts 15. They did not.

Adding Law to Grace

There is a danger when we attempt to please God by the works of the Law rather than rely on His grace alone, and the book of Galatians addresses this danger. Whenever we add anything from the Law to the work of Christ to be right with God, it diminishes what God has done for us, making Christ's work of no effect.

Galatians 5:4
Christ is become of no effect unto you, whosoever of you are justified by the law; ye are fallen from grace.

The tithe rightly falls under this category as it adds an ongoing requirement from the Law that people must do in order to maintain a right standing with God: either to receive His blessing or to avoid His chastening. Yet His righteousness has already been applied to the believer.

Romans 3:21-22

[3:21] But now the righteousness of God without the law is manifested, being witnessed by the law and the prophets; [22] Even **the righteousness of God** *which is* **by faith of Jesus Christ unto all and upon all them that believe:** for there is no difference:

If Jesus paid it all, how can anyone accuse God's people of owing God anything? He paid the price for our redemption, and we belong to Him. All that He has is ours and all that is ours is His. Against such a wonderful salvation that enables us to share in the blessings and fulness of God, measuring percentages seems rather trifling, does it not?

Tithing under the New Covenant:

Is Controversial

On the outset, the question as to whether or not New Testament believers are to tithe is controversial at best. Bible teachers, scholars, and preachers are divided over the issue. That fact alone should serve as a consideration for preachers and Bible teachers before they begin preaching on the dangers of robbing God; which also leads to another problem.

Breeds Blind Faith

Guilt-laden sermons geared toward the pocketbook leads many people to place their money into the offering plate with no real knowledge as to how it will be handled or where it will end up. It is common for people to say that they are doing their part and trust the Lord to use it as He sees fit. However, this kind of reasoning does not come from the Bible. In the Old Testament, the people were very well informed in all aspects regarding their tithes, offerings, and contributions of money. As we study the New Testament, we will find that the disciples who gave knew exactly where their gifts were going and how they would be put to use. They were also ensured that those who were entrusted with handling their offerings were reliable people. God does not want His people to give blindly, and those who practice blind giving are not obeying the Scriptures, for God has instructed otherwise.

Breeds Envy, Guilt and Pride

One of the major problems with the tithe is that it is something that not everyone *can* do, but is taught as something which is expected for everyone *to* do. Those who are able to tithe can get a sense of pride that they accomplished what God required of them. That in itself is sin. Pride is one of the things God hates (Proverbs 21:4). Furthermore, it leads to feelings of envy and guilt among those who struggle to make ends meet and need every last dollar to pay their bills. They might be told that they are in that condition because they are not tithing. Or they might also be advised that if they tithe, God will bless them financially. Teaching and expecting a requirement to tithe, which has no place in the New Testament, places a stumbling block in the path of our brothers and sisters in Christ.

Limits God's Resources

In regard to those whom God has gifted to give abundantly, the tithe doctrine sets limits on the resources available to a mere ten percent. The result is that the Spirit is quenched by false preaching and everyone loses. The potential giver loses out on Christ's promise of riches in heaven (Luke 12:33). Those who are in need here on earth lose out now because the tithe is used for building maintenance, new office machines, or other such expenses. Anything extra that God intended to be used for His glory is held back because the tithe has already been paid. Everything beyond ten percent can belong to the tither, who may spend it on selfish desires. The testimony of Jesus Christ does not surface for a witness to the world because the grace that should be revealed in us and through us has been effectively checked.

Breeds Contradiction

The contradictions are many, but here is an example. One key argument used to extract a ten percent offering from congregants is to point out that tithing occurred before the Law. Using Abraham as the prime example (because his tithe was before the Law), the attempt is to circumvent the Law and avoid the error addressed in Galatians (adding the Law to grace). Yet it is interesting that the accusation of "robbing God" is taken from Malachi where the tithe, not of Abraham, but of the Law (storehouse tithing) is the object. So the argument contradicts itself, for either the tithe of Abraham has nothing to do with the Law and is therefore free from the condemnation of Malachi, or the church is under the Law and the tithe of Abraham is merely a ploy to fool believers into subjection. It appears that the latter is the case, and both preacher and congregation have fallen into the same trap.

Leads to Empty Promises

The book of Malachi is used to convict congregations of robbing God for not tithing to their church. After the accusation and conviction, the preacher will challenge the congregation to test the LORD according to Malachi 3:10.

> **Malachi 3:10**
> [3:10] Bring ye all the tithes into the storehouse, that there may be meat in mine house, and prove me now herewith, saith the LORD of hosts, if I will not open you the windows of heaven, and pour you out a blessing, that *there shall* not *be room* enough *to receive it.*

There are those who would have us believe that the tithe leads to prosperity. Such a premise is misguided because it departs from God's original intent that the tithe be used to feed His people, and instead, creates a fee-collection system for the purchase of such things as choir robes or a new organ. This author has yet to see the level of blessing described in this passage upon any faithful tithe-giver, and finds most, if not all of them in approximately the same financial condition they were in twenty years ago.

Compromises the Grace of God

Romans 6:23

For the wages of sin *is* death; **but the gift of God *is* eternal life** through Jesus Christ our Lord.

The addition of a mandatory financial offering to the gift of God through Jesus Christ necessarily causes the free gift to no longer be free. Mandating a particular activity, such as tithing, to obtain God's blessings or to maintain God's favor sends the message that what Christ did for us was not enough. Yet Scripture says otherwise.

Romans 3:21-22

[3:21] But now the righteousness of God without the law is manifested, being witnessed by the law and the prophets; [22] Even **the righteousness of God *which is* by faith of Jesus Christ unto all and upon all them that believe:** for there is no difference

Galatians 3:10-12a

[3:10] For **as many as are of the works of the law are under the curse**: for it is written, **Cursed *is* every one that continueth not in all things** which are written in the book of the law to do them. [11] But that **no man is justified by the law** in the sight of God, *it is* evident: for, The just shall live by faith. [12a] And the law is not of faith

Galatians 5:4

[5:4] **Christ is become of no effect unto you,** whosoever of you are justified by the law; ye are fallen from grace.

Part II

New Testament

Giving

Introduction to New Testament Giving

A Different Standard

The New Testament is a different covenant with a completely different way of life than that presented in the Old. The Law is no longer the standard under the New Testament, for it has been done away in Christ, and has been nailed to the cross (Colossians 2:13-14). The old standard of the Law was also for a different economy, in which the tribes of Israel, having land and cattle, were to provide for the priests and Levites, as well as the needy living among them. The tithe, which was part of that provision, ended with that economy. And while God does not change, He is free to use different ways to accomplish His unchanging purposes.

A New Focus, a New Teaching

In the Old Testament, the promise and expectation of Israel was life in the Promised Land. Theirs was an earthly inheritance which entailed working the ground and raising livestock in order to provide sustenance for both family and community. It was God's intent for the kindness and generosity of His people to flourish in order that His blessings might flow abundantly among them. Yet because they chose not to follow the ways of God, and turned to other gods, the LORD removed His blessings; and instead of reaping a generous harvest, Israel reaped the wrath of God.

The New Testament has a different focus. The promise and expectation of the born-again believer in Jesus Christ is not of this world. Rather, it is an anticipation of eternal life in the kingdom of God.

Matthew 6:19-21

[6:19] Lay not up for yourselves treasures upon earth, where moth and rust doth corrupt, and where thieves break through and steal: [20] But lay up for yourselves treasures in heaven, where neither moth nor rust doth corrupt, and where thieves do not break through nor steal: [21] For where your treasure is, there will your heart be also.

2nd Timothy 2:11-12

[2:11] *It is* a faithful saying: For if we be dead with *him,* we shall also live with *him:* [12] If we suffer, we shall also reign with *him:* if we deny *him,* he also will deny us:

1st Corinthians 9:24-25

[9:24] Know ye not that they which run in a race run all, but one receiveth the prize? So run, that ye may obtain. [25] And every man that striveth for the mastery is temperate in all things. Now they *do it* to obtain a corruptible crown; but we an incorruptible.

Everlasting riches, varying degrees of power and authority, and reigning with Christ are a few of the eternal goals we seek to obtain. The Christian is to live a life worthy of attaining to these everlasting goals. This is a lifelong process and a work of God within us, without which it would be impossible.

Our focus is on God's kingdom, knowing that how we spend our days in this life will determine the outcome and rewards to be received in that everlasting kingdom. As such, the rules of engagement are completely different from those of Israel in the Old Testament.

Chapter 6

Christ's Doctrine of Giving

Jesus taught on the topic of giving on several occasions. Giving is important to God. It is part of His plan for His people. God is a giving God.

John 3:16a
For God so loved the world, that **he gave**....

To those who have been born into His kingdom, He is the Heavenly Father who desires for His children to be like Himself. In the following passages, we will examine some of Christ's instructions in regard to giving.

Matthew 5:42; 6:1-4: Giving, and Giving in Secret

These two passages from Matthew are part of what has become known as the Sermon on the Mount. Jesus went up on a mountain taught His disciples there (Matthew 5:1).

Matthew 5:42
[5:42] Give to him that asketh thee, and from him that would borrow of thee turn not thou away.

Matthew 6:1-4
[6:1] Take heed that ye do not your alms before men, to be seen of them: otherwise ye have no reward of your Father which is in heaven. [2] Therefore when thou doest *thine* alms, do not sound a trumpet before thee, as the hypocrites do in the synagogues and in the streets, that they may have glory of men. Verily I say unto you, they have their reward. [3] But when thou doest alms, let not thy left hand know what thy right hand doeth: [4] that thine alms may be in secret: and thy Father which seeth in secret himself shall reward thee openly.

Christ discusses giving at least twice in this sermon. His first reference (Matt. 5:42) is about how to deal with people who ask you for things. Jesus merely says we should give to them. The cross reference for this is Luke 6:30, where He also adds that if someone takes things from us (without even asking), we are not to ask for the return of the items taken.

On the surface, this seems to go too far. Yet when we consider the Source of all our blessings, it is not really too much at all. All things, including our own lives, belong to God. We brought nothing into this world, and we certainly cannot take anything with us when we go. To do as Jesus said in this passage reveals a proper understanding of God and His will, and reveals to others that you take His Word seriously. In many nations today, people are imprisoned, abused, beaten, and killed for believing in Jesus. What do your actions tell others of your faith in Christ?

> **Luke 16:10-11**
> [16:10] He that is faithful in that which is least is faithful also in much: and he that is unjust in the least is unjust also in much. [11] If therefore ye have not been faithful in the unrighteous mammon, who will commit to your trust the true *riches?*

In our second passage from Matthew's gospel (Matt. 6:1-4), Christ instructs us how to give when it is our desire to do so. When we come across someone in need, and want to help that person, He says that we are to do it **"in secret."** There are some very practical reasons for doing it this way. One reason is that you will avoid making the other person feel indebted to you. Another is that nobody will be able to accuse you of doing good things for publicity. But the best reason is the one Jesus Himself provides: **"thy Father which seeth in secret himself shall reward thee openly."**

Matthew 10:8: Why We Give

The context of Matthew 10 has Christ sending His twelve disciples to the lost sheep of Israel to preach the kingdom of God. He gave them power to heal and perform miracles. The last part of verse eight is our focus, for it is here that Jesus gives the reason for His expectation of liberality on the part of His disciples.

> **Matthew 10:8**
> [10:8] Heal the sick, cleanse the lepers, raise the dead, cast out devils: freely ye have received, freely give.

In that last phrase of Matthew 10:8, Jesus expressed the driving force and motivating factor for God's standard of giving: generosity. Freely we have received. Our very breath is not ours to keep, how much less the items we accumulate in this temporary existence? When we consider the generosity of God toward us, who are we to withhold anything at all? The new nature responds exactly as Jesus said it: **"freely ye have received, freely give."**

Luke 6:35: Godly Giving

Here Jesus instructs us on lending, and what kind of return we might expect on our loan.

> **Luke 6:35**
> [6:35] But love ye your enemies, and do good, and lend, hoping for nothing again; and your reward shall be great, and ye shall be the children of the Highest: for he is kind unto the unthankful and *to* the evil.

We are told to **"lend, hoping for nothing"** in return. Of course, that is not how this world operates. But then again, we are not supposed to be of this world. The honor of actually doing what Jesus tells us to do here is not without its consequence: **"and your reward shall be great, and ye shall be the children of the Highest."**

A proper understanding of grace received will desire to impart the gospel message in ways that reach beyond oral communication. The good news of Jesus Christ and His kingdom is not to be preached by word only. It is a way of life. It is a living demonstration of Christ working in us and through us, imparting to the world around us by word and deed the grace we have received. God gave, and we who are His children are to be like Him.

Luke 6:38: God's Economy

In this verse, Jesus promises that our generosity will be returned to us. Obeying the Lord is not without its rewards.

> **Luke 6:38**
> **[6:38] Give, and it shall be given unto you; good measure, pressed down, and shaken together, and running over, shall men give into your bosom. For with the same measure that ye mete withal it shall be measured to you again.**

Jesus assures that those who give will not go unrewarded. They will have things given to them. Note that the return is measured in direct proportion to the standard of the one who gives. In both quantity and quality, we will want to be giving our very best. Or better yet, His very best.

> **Proverbs 19:17**
> [9:17] He that hath pity upon the poor lendeth unto the LORD; and that which he hath given will he pay him again.

Luke 12:33: Giving All

Here is another passage where Jesus told His disciples how to give.

> **Luke 12:33**
> **[12:33] Sell that ye have, and give alms; provide yourselves bags which wax not old, a treasure in the heavens that faileth not, where no thief approacheth, neither moth corrupteth.**

In this verse, Christ told His disciples to sell the things they owned, and give the proceeds to help to the poor. We might consider this to be extreme. Jesus was an extremist. He gave all He had. And His encouragement toward His disciples to do the same is not without its rewards. God desires His people to reflect His kindness. Remember that the blessing of Israel was contingent on their faithfulness in providing for those in need (Deut. 14:28-29). God does not change, and there is a reward in giving. The latter part of the verse is a promise of an everlasting treasure to those who give abundantly.

Christ's Doctrine of Giving: How it Works

A Different Teaching

To say that Christ's teachings are unique would be an understatement. His precepts are radically different from any other teaching. Unlike the practical philosophies of this world, which emphasize self-sufficiency, or the so-called "village" mentality, Jesus Christ taught complete and total dependence on the Heavenly Father.

Our human nature tends to focus on the things that we have, or things we think we need. From that point we strive to seek ways to obtain things, and then go to great lengths to keep those things. Yet here is Jesus:

Mat 6:25-34

[6:25] Therefore I say unto you, **Take no thought for your life, what ye shall eat, or what ye shall drink; nor yet for your body, what ye shall put on.** Is not the life more than meat, and the body than raiment? [26] Behold the fowls of the air: for they sow not, neither do they reap, nor gather into barns; yet your heavenly Father feedeth them. Are ye not much better than they? [6:27] Which of you by taking thought can add one cubit unto his stature? [28] And why take ye thought for raiment? Consider the lilies of the field, how they grow; they toil not, neither do they spin: [29] and yet I say unto you, That even Solomon in all his glory was not arrayed like one of these. [30] Wherefore, if God so clothe the grass of the field, which today is, and tomorrow is cast into the oven, *shall he* not much more *clothe* you, O ye of little faith?
[6:31] Therefore take no thought, saying, "What shall we eat?" or, "What shall we drink?" or, "Wherewithal shall we be clothed?" [32] (For after all these things do the Gentiles seek.) For your heavenly Father knoweth that ye have need of all these things.

[6:33] **But seek ye first the kingdom of God, and his righteousness; and all these things shall be added unto you.** [6:34] Take therefore no thought for the morrow: for the morrow shall take thought for the things of itself. Sufficient unto the day *is* the evil thereof.

Christ tells us not to worry about things like eating, drinking or what clothing we will wear. In our way of thinking, food and drink are necessities. You can't live without these kinds of things. Yet Jesus says, **"Take no thought for your life**." What kind of teaching is this?

Seeking God's Kingdom

Remember that our goal is not of this world. We are not to be consumed with obtaining things. Our mission is to seek the **"kingdom of God, and His righteousness."** If we are doing that, Christ says that all these things will be added to us. So what does it mean to seek the kingdom of God? How do we obtain His righteousness?

Matthew 5:20
For I say unto you, That except your righteousness shall exceed *the righteousness* of the scribes and Pharisees, ye shall in no case enter into the kingdom of heaven.

According to these words of Jesus Christ, our entrance into God's kingdom hangs on whether or not we own a righteousness that exceeds that of the scribes and Pharisees. The scribes and Pharisees were very self-disciplined and worked hard to keep the commandments of God. If anyone on earth was considered righteous, it was them. Yet in all of their striving to make the grade, there was a problem. They were trusting in their own abilities.

The problem with human righteousness is that it grows out of a fallen human nature. As such, it is unacceptable to God. The Bible has some things to say about our righteousness.

Isaiah 64:6
[64:6] But we are all as an unclean *thing,* and all our righteousnesses *are* as filthy rags; and we all do fade as a leaf; and our iniquities, like the wind, have taken us away.

Romans 3:10
[3:10] As it is written, There is none righteous, no, not one:

When we understand that our righteousness does not measure up to God's standard, we are then in a position to realize that something is missing, and can then begin to seek the kind of righteousness Jesus mentioned: God's righteousness, which is available to anyone and everyone who trusts in Jesus Christ.

Romans 3:21-22
[3:21] But now the righteousness of God without the law is manifested, being witnessed by the law and the prophets; [22] **Even the righteousness of God** *which is* **by faith of Jesus Christ unto all and upon all them that believe**: for there is no difference:

Here you have it; a righteousness that descends directly from God, and He has to accept it because it is His righteousness. And He freely gives it to all who place their trust in Jesus Christ: "**unto all and upon all them that believe**." All you have to do is ask.

Matthew 7:7-8
[7:7] **Ask**, and it shall be given you; **seek**, and ye shall find; **knock**, and it shall be opened unto you: [8] for **every one** that asketh receiveth; and he that seeketh findeth; and to him that knocketh it shall be opened.

Having obtained God's righteousness through faith in Jesus Christ, access into God's kingdom is secure. But this is only the beginning; for once you receive Christ in your life, He begins to work on you from the inside.

Giving Like Jesus Gave

Jesus Christ gave His life so that you might have everlasting life. He did for you what you could not do for yourself. He did not have to do that, but it is in His nature to give. And once you receive Christ in your life, His nature begins to work inside you. His Spirit begins to abide within your being, transforming you into His likeness.

> **2nd Corinthians 3:18**
> [3:18] But we all, with open face beholding as in a glass the glory of the Lord, are changed into the same image from glory to glory, *even* as by the Spirit of the Lord.

Christ did not focus on the things of this world, but on the purpose of His Father in heaven. And we can be certain that as His nature grows within us, our focus will align with His. As we mature in Christ, we will reflect Him more perfectly to the world around us. In the process, we will find ourselves less likely to grasp those material possessions we once held dear, and look to Him who is eternal as we loosen our grip from the temporal.

Chapter 7

The Early Disciples

The book of Acts is known as the historical book of the New Testament, for it outlines the early history of the church after Christ had ascended into heaven. We have already read some of Christ's teachings about giving. Here in the book of Acts we will learn how the first disciples regarded the words of Jesus.

Acts 2:44-45; 4:34-35: The First Disciples and Giving

In Luke's gospel, Jesus told His disciples to sell the things they owned and give to the poor (Luke 12:33). After His death, burial, resurrection and ascension, the Holy Spirit descended upon the disciples and the church was born (Acts 2). The following accounts relate how the early disciples understood the words of Christ.

> Acts 2:44-45
> [2:44] And all that believed were together, and had all things common; [45] And sold their possessions and goods, and parted them to all *men*, as every man had need.
>
> Acts 4:32-35
> [4:32] And the multitude of them that believed were of one heart and of one soul: neither said any *of them* that ought of the things which he possessed was his own; but they had all things common. [33] And with great power gave the apostles witness of the resurrection of the Lord Jesus: and great grace was upon them all. [34] Neither was there any among them that lacked: for as many as were possessors of lands or houses sold them, and brought the prices of the things that were sold, [35] And laid *them* down at the apostles' feet: and distribution was made unto every man according as he had need.

According to both accounts in Acts, those who believed had all things common (2:44; 4:32). Those with possessions whether land or goods, sold them so that the proceeds could help those in need (2:45; 4:34-35). Note that they were not commanded to do what they did. The giving was voluntary, and based in an understanding that they were not the true owners the things they possessed (4:32).

Here we find no forced communism, but a proper recognition of ownership accompanied by selfless stewardship that elevated the needs of other believers above one's own desires. Here people valued the concern of God above their own concerns, and acted on it in a rare demonstration of what real love is all about. This is economics at work according to the kingdom of God. This is walking after the Spirit.

Unfortunately, this did not last. Persecution brought an end to it (Acts 8:1). But this is one of those times, and similar situations have occurred at various points in church history, where God's people completely gave themselves over to Christ. [20] It is on these occasions where Christianity shines brightest, that we get a glimpse of God's kingdom at work through His people.

Acts 4:36-37: The Example of Barnabus

Thus far, we've been given a general picture of how some of the wealthier disciples sold their possessions to relieve the needy among them. In this passage, we are provided a close up of one of these generous individuals who gave so abundantly. Joses, also known as Barnabus, is our example.

---

[20] Examples include St. Anthony, St. Francis of Assisi, and the Anabaptists of the sixteenth century.

Acts 4:36-37

[4:36] And Joses, who by the apostles was surnamed Barnabas, (which is, being interpreted, The son of consolation,) a Levite, *and* of the country of Cyprus, [37] having land, sold *it*, and brought the money, and laid *it* at the apostles' feet.

This is the first time we are introduced to Barnabus. He was among those who sold their possessions and gave the proceeds to meet the needs of other believers. Just as Jesus watched that widow who gave all she had (Luke 21:2-4), God sees the things we do and He knows our heart's intent. God saw Barnabus, and knew his heart. And later we find that God used Barnabus for greater things. We find him receiving Paul into the fellowship when the other disciples turned him away (Acts 9:26-27). We find him instrumental in the developing church at Antioch (Acts 11:22-24), and later with Paul on the first missionary journey (Acts 13:2-3). Barnabus is merely one close-up from among those who took Christ's words to heart. Yet had God chosen to exemplify any other such disciple, we would be right to expect something positive in that person's life as well.

God delights in providing examples. The parables of Jesus are stories given as examples to demonstrate spiritual truths and principles. Here we are given Barnabus as an example. It is as if God is using Barnabus to illustrate what can happen in our lives when we give all to Him.

Acts 5:1-11: The Example of Ananias and Sapphira

In contrast to Barnabus, we are also introduced to Ananias and Sapphira. They were not like Barnabus, although they attempted to appear like him.

Acts 5:1-11

[5:1] But a certain man named Ananias, with Sapphira his wife, sold a possession, [2] And kept back *part* of the price, his wife also being privy *to it,* and brought a certain part, and laid *it* at the apostles' feet. [3] But Peter said, Ananias, why hath Satan filled thine heart to lie to the Holy Ghost, and to keep back *part* of the price of the land? [4] Whiles it remained, was it not thine own? And after it was sold, was it not in thine own power? Why hast thou conceived this thing in thine heart? Thou hast not lied unto men, but unto God. [5:5] And Ananias hearing these words fell down, and gave up the ghost: and great fear came on all them that heard these things. [6] And the young men arose, wound him up, and carried *him* out, and buried *him.*

[5:7] And it was about the space of three hours after, when his wife, not knowing what was done, came in. [8] And Peter answered unto her, Tell me whether ye sold the land for so much? And she said, Yea, for so much. [9] Then Peter said unto her, How is it that ye have agreed together to tempt the Spirit of the Lord? Behold, the feet of them which have buried thy husband *are* at the door, and shall carry thee out. [10] Then fell she down straightway at his feet, and yielded up the ghost: and the young men came in, and found her dead, and, carrying *her* forth, buried *her* by her husband. [11] And great fear came upon all the church, and upon as many as heard these things.

While other disciples sold their possessions and gave the money they received to the apostles for distribution, these two attempted to deceive the church into thinking they were also doing that. Their reason for doing this is not addressed. Perhaps they were ambitious for some kind of status in the church and sought to achieve that by appearing spiritual. Or maybe they were just trying to blend in with the others. Whatever the case, they were not honest in what they did, as they kept back some of the money and made out as if they had given it all. We see what came of them, and unlike Barnabus, this is the last we will read about Ananias and Sapphira.

In regard to the tithe, how many have done something similar to Ananias and Sapphira? How many, because of condemning sermons, or peer pressure from fellow believers, pretend to give the tithe: not quite ten percent, but enough to blend in? This leads to a broader question. Who bears the greater guilt? Those who aren't tithing truthfully, or those who place them in that compromising position by the doctrines they preach? Maybe it's a good thing for us that God is no longer in the business of striking people dead where they stand for such sins as the one committed by Ananias and Sapphira.

Acts 6:1: The Daily Distribution

In Acts 6, we learn of a daily ministration that took place. We just read of the people who sold their possessions so that the proceeds could be distributed to help the needy among them. Here we find an example of how the disciples cared for those in need, particularly the widows.

> **Acts 6:1**
> **[6:1] And in those days, when the number of the disciples was multiplied, there arose a murmuring of the Grecians against the Hebrews, because their widows were neglected in the daily ministration.**

In this passage, we find that some of the widows were being neglected due to social discrimination. That situation is addressed later in the chapter, and God was glorified as a result (6:1-7).

Important to this study is the fact that the early disciples had established an organized procedure for providing for the widows. This provision for widows demonstrates the unchanging nature of God. We have seen that under the former economy of Israel, the Law contained provisions for the care of widows. Here we learn that the church continued to provide for them through this **"daily ministration."** The method is different, but God's purpose in providing for those in need did not change with the advent of Jesus Christ.

The Early Disciples: Final Analysis

We understand from the record in the book of Acts that the early disciples carried out the teachings of Jesus in regard to giving. They understood the purpose of God, and this is revealed by their actions. God's unchanging purpose in provision continued on in the New Covenant, yet in a new and different way from that of the Old Testament.

But we also find in this "paradise of God," the presence of a serpent. Unfaithfulness appeared in at least two areas. Ananias and Sapphira made an attempt at deception, and God dealt with them personally. The other area was bigoted in nature in that the Hellenistic widows were neglected at the daily distribution. This situation was handled by the choosing of seven men filled with the Spirit, resulting in the increase of the Word of God and multiplied disciples (Acts 6:7). From these two accounts we find that sin was still present, even among Christ's disciples; something every Christian knows all too well.

1st John 1:8
[1:18] If we say that we have no sin, we deceive ourselves, and the truth is not in us.

Chapter 8

Practical Instruction for New Testament Giving

On the topic of giving, instruction is not lacking in the New Testament. In fact, Scriptural instruction is very precise in this area on a variety of fronts, some of which we have already seen. As we move through the various teachings on support and provision, we will find that much if not all of it can be summed up in one word: attitude.

Philippians 2:3
[2:3] *Let* nothing *be done* through strife or vainglory; but in lowliness of mind let each esteem other better than themselves. [4] Look not every man on his own things, but every man also on the things of others.

Whether in giving or receiving, there is no room in for a self-serving attitude. The new birth is accompanied by a new nature that is diametrically opposed to the average human mindset. Human nature tells us to get. We are born with that mentality. That comes with being a baby. Contrary to our old way of thinking, the new nature tells us to give.

Ephesians 4:28
[4:28] Let him that stole steal no more: but rather let him labour, working with *his* hands the thing which is good, that he may have to give to him that needeth.

This verse admonishes those who once stole for a living to get a job. Yet it does not end with that. The former thief is to work not only for his own provision, but also that others might benefit from the fruit of his labor. The new nature is not merely about stopping a sinner from sinning. It's about producing good works in the life of a believer.

Ephesians 2:10
[2:10] For we are his workmanship, created in Christ Jesus unto good works, which God hath before ordained that we should walk in them.

Our entire way of life has been disrupted by Jesus Christ, who is at work within us to accomplish the will of the Father. The attitude of the new nature is one of servitude that places the needs of others (and particularly our brothers and sisters in Christ) above our own desires.

Galatians 6:10
[6:10] As we have therefore opportunity, let us do good unto all *men,* especially unto them who are of the household of faith.

James 2:14-17: Faith in Action

In following after good works, James offers some interesting insight.

James 2:14-17
[2:14] What *doth it* profit, my brethren, though a man say he hath faith, and have not works? Can faith save him? [15] If a brother or sister be naked, and destitute of daily food, [16] And one of you say unto them, Depart in peace, be *ye* warmed and filled; notwithstanding ye give them not those things which are needful to the body; what *doth it* profit? [17] Even so faith, if it hath not works, is dead, being alone.

Here we are informed that by not doing our part to provide for a brother or sister in need, our **"faith ... is dead."** It is of no use to go around professing the name of Jesus Christ if we are not backing up our profession by the things we do. People are watching, and for many in this world, we are the only Bible they will ever read.

Is your life in Christ real? If so, how do you demonstrate that reality to the world around you? Many people are willing to pray for others, but how many are willing to give when it will actually cost them something? It is not uncommon for people to find excuses when it comes to giving. Yet Jesus taught that we are to give, and it is the will of the Father that we take on His likeness.

Matthew 7:21
[7:21] Not everyone that saith unto me, Lord, Lord, shall enter into the kingdom of heaven; but he that doeth the will of my Father which is in heaven.

Note that James says nothing about giving a tithe. The focus of the Spirit is people, not organizations. Do not expect that God will commend your tithing to some Christian institution, when He has placed someone in need along your path and you chose not to help that person.

2nd Corinthians 5:10
[5:10] For we must all appear before the judgment seat of Christ; that every one may receive the things *done* in *his* body, according to that he hath done, whether *it be* good or bad.

1st John 3:16-18: Love in Action

James tests our faith by our works, and John tests our love using the same standard. While we are not saved by our works, it is through the things we do that we are revealed for who we are. As a tree is known by its fruit, we too will be known by the kind of fruit we produce.

1st John 3:16-18
[3:16] Hereby perceive we the love *of God*, because he laid down his life for us: and we ought to lay down *our* lives for the brethren. [17] But whoso hath this world's good, and seeth his brother have need, and shutteth up his bowels *of compassion* from him, how dwelleth the love of God in him? [18] My little children, let us not love in word, neither in tongue; but in deed and in truth.

John points out our motive for provision. Christ **"laid down His life for us."** Therefore we should **"lay down our**

lives for the brethren." To lay down our lives does not necessarily mean that we have to physically die. In this passage, the alternative, shutting up the "**bowels of compassion**," illustrates the point. In this context, laying down your life merely means to set your life aside: your desires, your schedule, your plans or business, your money or some other physical item, or whatever of "**this world's good**" you may have or hold dear.

It is like a man who had managed to save some money toward buying a piece of land, so that one day he might be able to build on it and live there. However, upon hearing of a family going through a difficult time, and understanding their situation, he gave very much of what he had saved toward helping them. He did not get the land, for he set himself aside and in effect died to his own desires to help that family. In a small way, he laid down his life for them. Yet because of what he did, the love of God was manifested. And there are promises that will be confirmed for this individual, for Christ Himself made those promises.

How many talk about love, but never show it in the way John describes above? God is a giving God. It is His desire that His children reflect His character.

> **John 13:35**
> [13:35] By this shall all *men* know that ye are my disciples, if ye have love one to another.

> **1st John 3:18**
> My little children, let us not love in word, neither in tongue; but in deed and in truth.

1ˢᵗ Timothy 6:17: The Rich

The Bible has a charge for those who have been blessed with material wealth.

> **1ˢᵗ Timothy 6:17-19**
> [6:17] Charge them that are rich in this world, that they be not high-minded, nor trust in uncertain riches, but in the living God, who giveth us richly all things to enjoy; [18] That they do good, that they be rich in good works, ready to distribute, willing to communicate; [19] Laying up in store for themselves a good foundation against the time to come, that they may lay hold on eternal life.

To be "**rich in good works**," according to this passage, is described as a state of readiness "**to distribute**." Geared toward people of wealth, this means to be always on the alert, looking for opportunity to do exactly what it says. Verse 19 tells us that those who carry out these instructions are "**laying up in store for themselves a good foundation against the time to come.**" This statement also provides us with a better understanding of these words of Jesus from Luke's gospel:

> **Luke 16:9**
> [16:9] And I say unto you, Make to yourselves friends of the mammon of unrighteousness; that, when ye fail, they may receive you into everlasting habitations.

The "**mammon of unrighteousness**" refers to riches, or money. While money, in and of itself, is morally neutral, there is nothing really good about worldly wealth either; hence it is called unrighteous. And yet, when put to use in ways that glorify God, such as paying some struggling individual's rent or electric bill (or, like our heavenly Father, providing something beyond all expectation), it will prove rewarding: here in this lifetime, and in the life to come.

God holds us accountable for the resources which He has committed to our trust. Jesus said that to whom much is given, much will be required (Luke 12:48). Sharing in the things God has given us is expected, and the fruit of good works should flow from the new life in Christ as naturally as an orange tree produces oranges. Giving maintains a high priority among the commands of Jesus Christ.

1st Timothy 5:3-12: Honoring Widows

In this passage we have the Scriptural instructions regarding church provision for widows. As we have already seen, this was an area of difficulty in the early church (Acts 6). Here in 1st Timothy we find sound teaching, informing us which widows are to receive support from the church and those who receive support from other sources. Also noteworthy is the meaning of the word, "honor."

> 1st Timothy 5:3-12
> [5:3] Honour widows that are widows indeed. [4] But if any widow have children or nephews, let them learn first to shew piety at home, and to requite their parents: for that is good and acceptable before God. [5] Now she that is a widow indeed, and desolate, trusteth in God, and continueth in supplications and prayers night and day. [6] But she that liveth in pleasure is dead while she liveth.
> [5:7] And these things give in charge, that they may be blameless. [8] But if any provide not for his own, and specially for those of his own house, he hath denied the faith, and is worse than an infidel.
> [5:9] Let not a widow be taken into the number under threescore years old, having been the wife of one man, [10] Well reported of for good works; if she have brought up children, if she have lodged strangers, if she have washed the saints' feet, if she have relieved the afflicted, if she have diligently followed every good work.
> [5:11] But the younger widows refuse: for when they have

begun to wax wanton against Christ, they will marry; [12] Having damnation, because they have cast off their first faith. [13] And withal they learn *to be* idle, wandering about from house to house; and not only idle, but tattlers also and busybodies, speaking things which they ought not. [14] I will therefore that the younger women marry, bear children, guide the house, give none occasion to the adversary to speak reproachfully.
[15] For some are already turned aside after Satan.
[5:16] If any man or woman that believeth have widows, let them relieve them, and let not the church be charged; that it may relieve them that are widows indeed.

The first sentence tells us to "**honour**" (King James spelling for honor) widows who are widows indeed. This word, honor, goes beyond a mere recognition of respect. To honor widows in the context of Scripture means to provide for them. The church is to honor (provide for) its widows.

While it is a Scriptural obligation for the church to provide for its widows, not every widow qualifies to receive this provision. The Bible lays out some detailed specifications for qualified widows. A widow worthy of church support is to have a proven track record of her faith toward God (5:5, 10). Widows with family do not qualify, for it is a family's obligation to see to the wellbeing of their widowed family members (5:4, 8, 16). Also, a widow under sixty is not to be considered for church provision (5:9, 11-15). Still, according to this passage, widows who meet the qualifications are entitled to provision at the expense of the body of Christ. Does your church provide for its widows, who are widows indeed?

Of the verses in the passage, verse 8 should be of particular interest to Christians. One who does not provide for his or her family is said to have "**denied the faith, and is worse than an infidel**." The current trend in our culture demonstrates a mass denial of the faith.

Ephesians 6:2-3: Honoring Parents

Continuing with the subject of those worthy of honor (provision), children are to be supportive of their parents. While this is something that has been lost in a major part of our culture in recent years, it is still practiced by some.

It is within the standard of natural affection that children, once grown, would desire to provide something in return for those who raised them.

> **Ephesians 6:2-3**
> **[6:2] Honour thy father and mother; (which is the first commandment with promise) [3] That it may be well with thee, and thou mayest live long on the earth.**

This passage has a commandment from the Old Testament that has been carried over and written into the New. God does not change. His purposes do not change. And while He uses different means to fulfill His purposes, here we find a method that remains constant; for this is a standard of love, which was woven into the fabric of family from the beginning.

Unfortunately, our fallen nature tends to lean toward our own understanding and away from God's purposes. By the time of Jesus' earthly ministry, for example, the scribes and Pharisees had effectively interpreted their own views into God's Law, and created doctrines which they expected the people to follow. In doing this, they obscured God's original intent for the good of His people.

> **Mark 7:9-13**
> [7:9] And he said unto them, Full well ye reject the commandment of God, that ye may keep your own tradition. [10] For Moses said, Honour thy father and thy mother; and, Whoso curseth father or mother, let him die the death: [11] But ye say, If a man shall say to his father or mother, *It is* Corban,

that is to say, a gift, by whatsoever thou mightest be profited by me; *he shall be free.* [12] And ye suffer him no more to do ought for his father or his mother; [13] Making the word of God of none effect through your tradition, which ye have delivered: and many such like things do ye.

In the overall of this passage, we find that honoring parents meant that the children should also provide for them. But Jesus tells us that what should have gone toward honoring parents was being taken from them under the name of "**Corban**." To call something *Corban* meant that it was a gift set apart as an offering to God.[21] An adult child, choosing not to honor his parents, could easily escape punishment for his offense by declaring *Corban* on the goods in question. This kind of robbery can occur under a variety of scenarios.

Suppose for example, an individual had made an agreement to honor his parents with a specific gift, but then adversity comes between him and his parents. Because of their disagreement, he refuses to honor them. When brought before the judges, he says the gift is *Corban.* Nobody is going to argue "**a gift**" dedicated to God, so he goes unpunished. The end result is that the parents are not honored and the commandment of God has been undermined. They had made "**the word of God of none effect through** [their] **tradition**."

Another situation might be something similar to what goes on today with the teaching of the tithe, in which ten percent of a church member's income is an automatic *Corban*: set aside for God to be given to the church. Yet if that amount infringes in any way on what should be used to honor one's parents, then this same condemnation of Jesus might easily apply today. For unlike the tithe, which was specifically for Israel under the Law and does

---

[21] Vine, W. F.: *Vine's Expository Dictionary of New Testament Words*, Oliphants, Ltd., 1952, p.240. Hereafter referred to as *Vine's*.

not apply today, honoring parents is one command that is literally carried over into the New Testament.

> **Matthew 15:9**
> [15:9] But in vain they do worship me, teaching *for* doctrines the commandments of men.

We would do well to honor our parents.

1st Timothy 5:17-18: Honoring Elders

Honoring (providing for) certain individuals includes the elders of the church. Elders in this context are not merely older men in the church. These men are the spiritual leaders of the church.

> **1st Timothy 5:17-18**
> [5:17] Let the elders that rule well be counted worthy of double honour, especially they who labour in the word and doctrine. [18] For the scripture saith, Thou shalt not muzzle the ox that treadeth out the corn. And, The labourer *is* worthy of his reward.

The **"elders that rule well"** are to be **"counted worthy of double honor."** The church should ensure that the elders receive a special measure of care and provision. The early churches normally had a plurality of elders (Acts 14:23; 20:17; James 5:14). Some of these leaders, like Paul, may have worked for a living (Acts 18:3; 1st Corinthians 9:6, 14-15). But those who **"rule well"** and **"labor in the word and doctrine"** are definitely to receive support from the church.

> **1 Corinthians 9:13-14**
> [9:13] Do ye not know that they which minister about holy things live *of the things* of the temple? And they which wait at the altar are partakers with the altar? [14] Even so hath the Lord ordained that they which preach the gospel should live of the gospel.

How the elders are supported will certainly vary depending on the situation. While it was not God's intention that church leaders live in luxury at the expense of poor church members, it was also not His intent that elders should "**labor in the word and doctrine**" without some form of provision.

1ˢᵗ Corinthians 16:1-3: Collections

The following passage refers to a collection that Paul was taking for the poor saints in Jerusalem (see also Romans 15:25-26). For us today, it provides some Scriptural principles for collective giving in the church.

> **1ˢᵗ Corinthians 16:1-3**
> **[16:1] Now concerning the collection for the saints, as I have given order to the churches of Galatia, even so do ye. [2] Upon the first *day* of the week let every one of you lay by him in store, as *God* hath prospered him, that there be no gatherings when I come. [3] And when I come, whomsoever ye shall approve by *your* letters, them will I send to bring your liberality unto Jerusalem.**

There are at least three principles spelled out in these verses in regard to giving and collections: preparation, ability, and approval. In "**preparation**," a certain day was appointed for setting aside what each person had to offer. In this case it was "**the first *day* of the week**" (16:2). By setting aside a certain time and place for collecting money or goods for a cause, people can be adequately prepared when it is time to give. And when the time comes for the recipient to receive what is to be given, the items have already been set aside for that purpose.

People were to give according to their ability: "**as God hath prospered**" (16:2). While some might want to make a case out of this for some kind of percentage, this passage makes no such statement. Some could obviously afford to give more than others, but there is no standard amount or percentage. They were merely to give **"as God hath prospered"** them.

Those entrusted with the care and handling of the offering had to meet the approval of the church: **"whomsoever ye shall approve by _your_ letters"** (16:3). The Bible does not teach blind giving. The people at Corinth knew that the money was going to help **"the saints,"** and those who would handle the offering had to meet their approval. The New Testament affirms honesty, not only in the sight of God, but also in the sight of men.

> 2nd Corinthians 8:20-21
> [8:20] Avoiding this, that no man should blame us in this abundance which is administered by us: [21] providing for honest things, not only in the sight of the Lord, but also in the sight of men.

2nd Corinthians 8:1-7: A Giving Attitude

Here we are given instruction by example. In this passage, God has chosen the assemblies in Macedonia to provide for us a living parable in demonstrating His will when it comes to giving. What is God like? Check out the Macedonian believers.

> 2nd Corinthians 8:1-7
> [8:1] Moreover, brethren, we do you to wit of the grace of God bestowed on the churches of Macedonia; [2] How that in a great trial of affliction the abundance of their joy and their deep poverty abounded unto the riches of their liberality. [3] For to _their_ power, I bear record, yea, and beyond _their_ power _they were_ willing of themselves; [4] Praying us with much intreaty that we would receive the gift, and _take upon us_ the fellowship of the ministering to the saints. [5] And _this they did,_ not as we hoped, but first gave their own selves to the Lord, and unto us by the will of God. [6] Insomuch that we desired Titus, that as he had begun, so he would also finish in you the same grace also. [7] Therefore, as ye abound in every _thing, in_ faith, and

utterance, and knowledge, and *in* all diligence, and *in* your love to us, *see* that ye abound in this grace also.

Here we are told that giving is a **"grace"** (verses 1 and 7). Grace means "unmerited favor."[22] In the first verse, our attention is focused on the unmerited favor of God toward the churches of Macedonia. The following verses (2-5) describe the outworking of God's unmerited favor through the Macedonian believers by their generosity as witnessed by Paul and those who were with him. In the last two verses, the Corinthian believers are afforded the opportunity to demonstrate the same outworking of God's unmerited favor. Giving is a grace.

The people in the churches of Macedonia were not only willing to give, they insisted: **"Praying us with much intreaty that we would receive the gift."** This is the attitude God desires from His people. When it comes to supporting our brothers and sisters in Christ, we should be more than generous.

Note that these believers **"first gave their own selves to the Lord"** (8:5). This is the definition of holiness. To be holy means to be set aside for the use of God.[23]

2nd Corinthians 8:8-11: Graceful Giving

We now move from the Macedonian example to the Corinthian challenge (and a challenge for us as well). The Corinthians had made a commitment, and they are challenged to carry out that commitment.

2nd Corinthians 8:8-11
[8:8] I speak not by commandment, but by occasion of the forwardness of others, and to prove the sincerity of your love. [9] For ye know the grace of our Lord Jesus Christ, that,

---

[22] The grace of God toward us is revealed in His free gift of everlasting life through Jesus Christ. Also referred to as **G**od's **R**iches **A**t **Ch**rist's Expense. See also *Vine's*, pp. 169-171 for a more expanded definition for grace.

[23] See *Vine's*, pp. 225-27.

though he was rich, yet for your sakes he became poor, that ye through his poverty might be rich. [10] And herein I give *my* advice: for this is expedient for you, who have begun before, not only to do, but also to be forward a year ago. [11] Now therefore perform the doing *of it;* that as *there was* a readiness to will, so *there may be* a performance also out of that which ye have.

We do not want to miss the phrase in eighth verse: "**I speak not by commandment**." Graceful giving is never by commandment. The decision to give is completely up to the individual; otherwise it is no longer grace. In this passage we learn that the believers at Corinth had already made a commitment to give something (8:10), and Paul is testing their **"sincerity"** by the example set by the Macedonians: **"the forwardness of others"** (8:8).

We can also test our sincerity by these words of Scripture. Whenever we make a commitment, we are expected to **"perform the doing of it"** (8:11). God is good on His promises, and we who are His children are to reflect His character in our in our lives. Jesus Christ is our example (8:9). It is for our sakes **"he became poor,"** that we **"might be rich,"** and that His grace might work in us to accomplish His purpose through us. How is the grace of Jesus Christ working in your life?

2ⁿᵈ Corinthians 8:12-15: Equality in Giving

Proceeding in the same chapter, we learn that giving is not to be burdensome.

2nd Corinthians 8:12-15
[8:12] For if there be first a willing mind, *it is* accepted according to that a man hath, *and* not according to that he hath not. [13] For *I mean* not that other men be eased, and ye burdened: [14] But by an equality, *that* now at this time your abundance *may be a supply* for their want, that their abundance also may be *a supply* for your want: that there

may be equality: [15] As it is written, He that *had gathered* much had nothing over; and he that *had gathered* little had no lack.

Here we are told that when we give, we must first have "**a willing mind**." If someone is not willing, that person should not give. But from someone who is willing, the gift is to be "**accepted**" only according to what he or she can actually afford: "**according to that a man hath, *and* not according to that he hath not**" (8:12). No one should receive an offering to the injury of the one giving the offering. There is to be a balance ("**equality**") to prevent some from profiting at the expense of others: "**For *I mean* not that other men be eased, and ye burdened**" (8:13). There are some preachers who need to learn this lesson.

2nd Corinthians 8:16-24: Providing for Honest Things

These final verses in chapter 8 demonstrate that those who receive support are to be open and honest with those who provide the support. There is no such thing as blind faith when it comes to giving according to the New Testament.

2nd Corinthians 8:16-24
[8:16] But thanks *be* to God, which put the same earnest care into the heart of Titus for you. [17] For indeed he accepted the exhortation; but being more forward, of his own accord he went unto you. [18] And we have sent with him the brother, whose praise *is* in the gospel throughout all the churches; [19] And not *that* only, but who was also chosen of the churches to travel with us with this grace, which is administered by us to the glory of the same Lord, and *declaration of* your ready mind: [20] Avoiding this, that no man should blame us in this abundance which is administered by us: [21] Providing for honest things, not only in the sight of the Lord, but also in the sight of men. [22] And we have sent with them our brother, whom we

have oftentimes proved diligent in many things, but now much more diligent, upon the great confidence which *I have* in you. [23] Whether *any do enquire* of Titus, *he is* my partner and fellow-helper concerning you: or our brethren *be enquired of, they are* the messengers of the churches, *and* the glory of Christ. [24] Wherefore shew ye to them, and before the churches, the proof of your love, and of our boasting on your behalf.

The Corinthians knew the purpose of their offering, as they had made a previous commitment to provide the support. But could they trust the people who handled the money? Here we find that Paul went through great lengths to convince the Corinthians that their gifts would be committed to reliable men. They already knew Titus, and the other man who accompanied Titus was not only commended by **"all the churches,"** but was also **"chosen of the churches"** (8:18-19). It is God's desire that His people provide **"for honest things, not only in the sight of the Lord, but also in the sight of men"** (8:21).

Through the inspired Word, the Holy Spirit teaches us that we are not to give blindly. Many people today give without knowing where the money is going or how it is being used. But according to God's Word, we should know and approve of how our gifts are used, and be assured that those handling our offering are trustworthy.

2nd Corinthians 9:1-5: Fulfilling Your Commitment

Continuing where chapter 8 leaves off, the first five verses of chapter 9 encourage the Corinthian believers to make good on the promise they had made the year before (2nd Cor. 8:10-11).

2nd Corinthians 9:1-5
[9:1] For as touching the ministering to the saints, it is superfluous for me to write to you: [2] For I know the forwardness of your mind, for which I boast of you to them

of Macedonia, that Achaia was ready a year ago; and your zeal hath provoked very many. [3] Yet have I sent the brethren, lest our boasting of you should be in vain in this behalf; that, as I said, ye may be ready: [4] Lest haply if they of Macedonia come with me, and find you unprepared, we (that we say not, ye) should be ashamed in this same confident boasting. [5] Therefore I thought it necessary to exhort the brethren, that they would go before unto you, and make up beforehand your bounty, whereof ye had notice before, that the same might be ready, as *a matter of* bounty, and not as *of* covetousness.

The believers at Corinth were so enthusiastic in their commitment to provide for the needs of the saints that Paul boasted of them to the churches in Macedonia. Their enthusiasm inspired others to do the same (9:1-2). Now that the time has arrived to make good on their promise, Paul is sending some men in advance so that they can be prepared and fulfill their obligation (3-5).

When we make commitments, God expects that we fulfill them. When others hear of what we intend to do, we are to be solid. God is dependable. What He says, He does. If we are going to reflect His likeness to this world, cheap talk is not to be one of our defining characteristics. What we say can either inspire others, or make us a laughing stock.

What message are you sending to the world around you? Is Jesus Christ glorified in the things you do? Do you make good on your commitments? Do you generate the kind of fruit that glorifies your Heavenly Father?

Matthew 7:20-21
[7:20] Wherefore, by their fruits ye shall know them. [21] Not everyone that saith unto me, Lord, Lord, shall enter into the kingdom of heaven; but he that doeth the will of my Father which is in heaven.

114

John 15:8
[15:8] Herein is my Father glorified, that ye bear much fruit; so shall ye be my disciples.

2nd Corinthians 9:6-7: Sowing and Reaping

Continuing in 2nd Corinthians 9, we find the New Testament standard for giving here in verses 6 and 7.

2nd Corinthians 9:6-7
[9:6] But this *I say*, He which soweth sparingly shall reap also sparingly; and he which soweth bountifully shall reap also bountifully. [7] Every man according as he purposeth in his heart, *so let him give;* not grudgingly, or of necessity: for God loveth a cheerful giver.

Here we find no mandated percentage or an expected amount from those who give. The New Testament principle for giving is based on both the attitude and generosity of the giver. A proper reflection of God's love and grace would be to give abundantly without reservation, for that is within the nature and character of God, who gives abundantly and pardons freely. And the promise is that those who give abundantly will also reap abundantly ("**bountifully**"), while those who give "**sparingly**" should expect little in return.

2nd Corinthians 9:7 is probably one of the most violated passages in the New Testament. When ministers demand the tithe from their congregations, the offering becomes a "**necessity**." It is no longer "**every man as he purposeth in his heart**," but as the preacher purposes for every man. As such, it might easily be given "**grudgingly**" by some due to the fact that it is no longer an offering from a "**cheerful giver**," but something closer to a tax imposed externally by the minister.

The New Testament standard for measurement is grace. It is measured by the unmerited favor of every man, who cheerfully gives freely, **"according as he purposeth in his heart**."

> Luke 6:38
> [16:38] Give, and it shall be given unto you; good measure, pressed down, and shaken together, and running over, shall men give into your bosom. **For with the same measure that ye mete withal it shall be measured to you again.**

1st Corinthians 9:1-18: Attitude of the Receiver

We have been in 2nd Corinthians 9, and now we turn to 1st Corinthians 9. In this passage, Paul confirms God's provision for church leaders as spelled out in 1st Timothy 5:17-18. Yet while validating congregational support for those who minister, his own example provides a pattern to be followed by those on the receiving end.

> 1st Corinthians 9:1-18
> [9:1] Am I not an apostle? Am I not free? Have I not seen Jesus Christ our Lord? Are not ye my work in the Lord? [2] If I be not an apostle unto others, yet doubtless I am to you: for the seal of mine apostleship are ye in the Lord.
> [9:3] Mine answer to them that do examine me is this, [4] Have we not power to eat and to drink? [5] Have we not power to lead about a sister, a wife, as well as other apostles, and *as* the brethren of the Lord, and Cephas? [6] Or I only and Barnabas, have not we power to forbear working?
> [9:7] Who goeth a warfare any time at his own charges? Who planteth a vineyard, and eateth not of the fruit thereof? Or who feedeth a flock, and eateth not of the milk of the flock? [8] Say I these things as a man? Or saith not the law the same also? [9] For it is written in the Law of Moses, Thou shalt not muzzle the mouth of the ox that treadeth out the corn. Doth God take care for oxen? [10] Or saith he *it* altogether for our sakes? For our sakes, no doubt, *this* is written: that he that

116

ploweth should plow in hope; and that he that thresheth in hope should be partaker of his hope. [9:11] If we have sown unto you spiritual things, *is it* a great thing if we shall reap your carnal things? [12] If others be partakers of *this* power over you, *are* not we rather? Nevertheless we have not used this power; but suffer all things, lest we should hinder the gospel of Christ. [9:13] Do ye not know that they which minister about holy things live *of the things* of the temple? and they which wait at the altar are partakers with the altar? [14] Even so hath the Lord ordained that they which preach the gospel should live of the gospel. [15] But I have used none of these things: neither have I written these things, that it should be so done unto me: for *it were* better for me to die, than that any man should make my glorying void. [16] For though I preach the gospel, I have nothing to glory of: for necessity is laid upon me; yea, woe is unto me, if I preach not the gospel! [17] For if I do this thing willingly, I have a reward: but if against my will, a dispensation *of the gospel* is committed unto me. [18] What is my reward then? *Verily* that, when I preach the gospel, I may make the gospel of Christ without charge, that I abuse not my power in the gospel.

Here we are exposed to the kind of attitude God desires from those He chooses to shepherd His flock. As an apostle of Jesus Christ, Paul shared the same rights that the other apostles were enjoying (9:1-5). Apparently the others were supported by the churches while Paul and Barnabus worked to support themselves (9:6). Arguing from sound reasoning as well from as the Law (vss. 7-13), Paul demonstrates that he is well within his rights to be supported by his ministry, summing it all up by the fact that the **"Lord ordained that they which preach the gospel should live of the gospel"** (9:14).

And yet, while Paul owned the right to receive his support from those to whom he ministered, he chose to forfeit that right, **"lest [he] should hinder the gospel of Christ"** (9:12). And although this passage reveals God's purpose in providing for His ministers, Paul's example still shines through: **"neither have I written these things, that it should be so done unto me"** (9:15). Others may partake of their right to provision according to God's plan and purpose, but Paul's example demonstrates a deeper commitment; one that searches the depths of God's love.

1st Corinthians 9:18

[9:18] What is my reward then? *Verily* that, when I preach the gospel, I may make the gospel of Christ without charge, that I abuse not my power in the gospel.

Of all the apostles, God chose Paul to exemplify His desire for His people down through the centuries. Paul made it a point not to burden the church with his material necessities. God's full will also includes our attitudes. What we have in this passage reveals Paul's personal attitude, which is also an example for us to follow.

2nd Thessalonians 3:8-9

[3:8] Neither did we eat any man's bread for nought; but wrought with labour and travail night and day, that we might not be chargeable to any of you: [9] Not because we have not power, **but to make ourselves an ensample unto you to follow us.**

Throughout the New Testament, we are reminded to follow Paul's example.

1st Corinthians 11:1

[11:1] **Be ye followers of me**, even as I also *am* of Christ.

Philippians 3:17

[3:17] Brethren, **be followers together of me**, and mark them which walk so as **ye have us for an ensample.**

Philippians 4:9

[4:9] **Those things, which ye have both learned, and received, and heard, and seen in me, do:** and the God of peace shall be with you.

In closing this section, it must be remembered that Paul understood himself as the exception rather than the rule. He admitted that the course he chose was different from what the other apostles and church leaders were doing in this area of provision (1st Cor. 9:5-6). But in the overall picture presented in this passage, we have a demonstrated *attitude* that placed concern for the gospel and the church over and above personal concerns of food, housing and raiment. That is the example, and God delights in providing examples for us to follow.

Practical Instruction
For New Testament Giving:
Final Analysis

New Testament Giving Exhibits Faith and Love

Our faith, as well as our love is tested in our giving. The passages out of James and 1st John awaken our awareness that God expects for His love to be seen in us by those around us as we demonstrate our faith in Him through the things we do. According to 1st John, if we have the means to provide for a brother or sister in need, yet for some reason decide not to help that person, we do not have the love of God abiding in us (1st John 3:17). James tells us that the kind of faith that refuses to help that person is dead, because living faith is made known through our works (James 2:15-17). As God provides opportunity through others, we should be ready to give, and give abundantly. People are watching, and Jesus said that they will be able to recognize us as His disciples by our love for one another (John 13:35). We show our love through the things we do; and it is in these things that our faith shines through.

> **1st John 3:18**
> My little children, let us not love in word, neither in tongue; but in deed and in truth.

The Gift of Giving

Those who have been blessed with material wealth are instructed to be ready to share (1st Tim. 6:17-19). Just as God gifts teachers and expects that they use their gift for the edification of the church, He expects those gifted financially to use what He gave them for the same purpose, that Christ may be glorified.

Romans 12:6-8a

[12:6] **Having then gifts differing according to the grace that is given to us,** whether prophecy, *let us prophesy* according to the proportion of faith; [7] Or ministry, *let us wait* on *our* ministering: or he that teacheth, on teaching; [8a] Or he that exhorteth, on exhortation: **he that giveth,** *let him do it* **with simplicity;**

1st Corinthians 4:7

[4:7] For who maketh thee to differ *from another?* And what hast thou that thou didst not receive? Now if thou didst receive *it,* why dost thou glory, as if thou hadst not received *it?*

Some Christians have trouble identifying their spiritual gifts. A person of wealth should have no problem acknowledging at least one potential gift: the gift of giving. And for some poor soul, that might also mean a miracle.

Recipients of the Gift

The New Testament lists at least two specific categories of those who are to receive support at the expense of the church, and one that is not so specific. The church is charged to support qualified widows, as well as its elders who labor in the Word (1st Tim. 5:3-12, 17-18). The other category is simply those in need, such as the saints for whom Paul took a collection (2nd Cor. 8-9).

Outside the church, children are to honor (provide for) their own parents (Matt. 15:4-6; Eph. 6:2-3). This would also include children that have a parent who is a widow (1st Tim. 5:4, 8, 16). Widows with children are not to be supported by the church. It is the job of the widow's children to care for her.

The attitude of those on the receiving is exemplified by Paul's attitude (1st Cor. 9:1-18). Christians who truly place the needs of others above their own desires will not want to be a burden on other believers (Phil. 2:3-4; 2nd Cor. 8:13). However, we all need help in many areas, and somebody has to be the Jesus in need in order for His love to shine through the faithfulness of other believers. At some point, we all fill the part of **"the least of these my brethren"** (Matt. 25:40). And it is through these occasions that we obtain testimonies for Jesus Christ and bear witness to His ongoing work in this world (Acts 1:8; Rev. 12:11).

Please take note that there is no instruction in the New Testament in regard to financing denominational church organizations, buildings, associational programs, organs, pianos, or other such expenses. God is in the business of helping people who cannot help themselves, and then equipping those very people to do the same so that His grace shines through them as vessels of His glory.

Collections and the Offering

There are times when it becomes necessary to collect funds from an entire assembly of believers. It is during these times that a church can really honor our Lord. If a commitment is made on a certain amount, or leaves an impression of great generosity, the church is to make good on her commitment so that the testimony of Jesus is not compromised. In such times when mass collections are necessary, the church should also be informed as to how the funds are to be used, and assured that the money will make it to its proper destination for its intended purpose. It is not God's will for His people to give blindly (1st Cor. 16:3; 2nd Cor. 8:16-21).

By virtue of tradition, the offering has been placed within the worship service as a time of individual sacrifice. This is something not easily changed. People want to give unto God something of value, and the offering provides that opportunity. The New Testament has no teaching as such, for giving to God is found in how we give to those He brings into our lives, and particularly those of the household of faith (Gal. 6:10).

Proverbs 19:17
He that hath pity upon the poor lendeth unto the LORD; and that which he hath given will he pay him again.

Contrary to popular belief, true worship and sacrifice is not something that takes place on Sunday morning (or on the Sabbath, for those who prefer Saturday). To worship God in spirit and in truth means to live everyday to the glory of God. And sacrifice is not something we put in the offering plate. We are the sacrifice.

Romans 12:1-2
[12:1] I beseech you therefore, brethren, by the mercies of God, that ye present your bodies a living sacrifice, holy, acceptable unto God, *which is* your reasonable service. [2] And be not conformed to this world: but be ye transformed by the renewing of your mind, that ye may prove what *is* that good, and acceptable, and perfect, will of God.

Regarding giving, the New Testament directive begins and ends with helping people. Should a congregation choose to purchase or rent a facility, they commit to its expenses. The cost, however, will hamper the ability of the church to carry out Christ's commandment in helping those in need. Whatever the case, a Christian should know how his or her money is being used, and sacrificial generosity in this area is to be encouraged.

Graceful Giving

The Bible is clear that New Testament giving is not by commandment (2nd Cor. 8:8). It is not a required percentage. New Testament giving is a grace (2nd Cor. 8:1, 7). Grace means "unmerited favor." The only way we can accurately reflect the unmerited favor we have received from the hand of God is to "go and do likewise" (Luke 10:30-37).

Grace came to us merely by our hearing and believing the gospel. Grace is conferring, without reservation, favorable actions toward someone who does not deserve it, or may even (as in our own case with God) deserve the complete opposite. Grace is completely and totally determined by the one who administers the free gift. Any external imposition mandating what is given is not of grace.

Graceful giving is not without its rewards. Whether in this life or in the life to come, God promises that the good things done by His people will not go unrewarded.

> **Luke 6:35-36**
> [35] But love ye your enemies, and **do good, and lend, hoping for nothing again; and your reward shall be great,** and ye shall be the children of the Highest: for he is kind unto the unthankful and *to* the evil. [36] Be ye therefore merciful, as your Father also is merciful.

> **Luke 6:38**
> [6:38] **Give, and it shall be given unto you; good measure, pressed down, and shaken together, and running over, shall men give into your bosom.** For with the same measure that ye mete withal it shall be measured to you again.

> **1st Corinthians 15:58**
> [15:58] Therefore, my beloved brethren, be ye stedfast, unmoveable, always abounding in the work of the Lord, forasmuch as **ye know that your labour is not in vain in the Lord.**

New Testament Giving:
Some Afterthoughts

The Dilemma of New Testament Giving

An advantage to teaching a percentage of income for a standard of giving is that it is something we can grasp. We can figure it out and know what it is. For those who cannot make it to that standard, it might become a goal. For those who are able to attain the goal, they can feel good about it, for they have done what they have been taught that God requires. But God is not bound to the ideas or standards that men read into His Word.

New Testament giving is in tune with the grace of God. It brings us to a crisis of belief. We have to choose between God's provision and our own understanding. It is personal, and like the decision that brings us to salvation, there is no mistaking the will of God. There is sacrifice involved, and loss. And many times others cannot know about our sacrifices because Jesus teaches that our giving is to be done in secret (Matt. 6:3-4). Yet there is also a promise of greater things to those who follow the ways of God. That is what grace is all about.

Philippians 2:5-9
[2:5] **Let this mind be in you,** which was also in Christ Jesus: [6] Who, being in the form of God, thought it not robbery to be equal with God: [7] But made himself of no reputation, and took upon him the form of a servant, and was made in the likeness of men: [8] And being found in fashion as a man, he humbled himself, and became obedient unto death, even the death of the cross. [9] **Wherefore God also hath highly exalted him,** and given him a name which is above every name:

The choice is not really about giving up possessions. You cannot keep them anyway. The decision is God-centered. God is aiming for your heart. Do you really love God? Do you really know Him at all? Is He real to you? Is He waiting in secret, to see the fruit of your faith in your time of trial? These are genuine questions that confront us when we face a real crisis about giving. "What would Jesus do?" That was the popular question to ask not so long ago. But rather, the question should always be, what does He expect?

> **Acts 20:35**
> [20:35] I have shewed you all things, how that so labouring ye ought to support the weak, and to **remember the words of the Lord Jesus, how he said, It is more blessed to give than to receive.**

New Testament Giving is People-Oriented

At every instance when giving is mentioned in the New Testament, it always regards helping others (Matt. 5:42; 1st John 3:17; etc.). New Testament giving is people-oriented. God is concerned about individuals, and His church is not built with bricks or mortar. We who belong to Christ are His church, and are bound together by His Spirit who abides within each of us. Through the Spirit of Christ, we are one body. And in whatever ways God has enabled us, we are to use our abilities to edify one another.

> **1st Corinthians 12:4-7**
> [12:4] Now there are diversities of gifts, but the same Spirit. [5] And there are differences of administrations, but the same Lord. [6] And there are diversities of operations, but it is the same God which worketh all in all. [7] But the manifestation of the Spirit is given to every man to profit withal.

A Standard for Judgment

Matthew 25:31-46 provides a literal example for at least one of God's standards by which people will be judged. Certainly those in Christ are not condemned, and judgment passes over where the blood of the Lamb has been applied. Yet here we find Jesus separating mankind into two different groups, as a shepherd separates sheep from goats.

> Matthew 25:31-46
>
> [25:31] When the Son of man shall come in his glory, and all the holy angels with him, then shall he sit upon the throne of his glory: [32] And before him shall be gathered all nations: and he shall separate them one from another, as a shepherd divideth *his* sheep from the goats: [33] And he shall set the sheep on his right hand, but the goats on the left.
>
> [25:34] Then shall the King say unto them on his right hand, Come, ye blessed of my Father, inherit the kingdom prepared for you from the foundation of the world: [35] For I was an hungred, and ye gave me meat: I was thirsty, and ye gave me drink: I was a stranger, and ye took me in: [36] Naked, and ye clothed me: I was sick, and ye visited me: I was in prison, and ye came unto me.
>
> [25:37] Then shall the righteous answer him, saying, Lord, when saw we thee an hungred, and fed *thee?* or thirsty, and gave *thee* drink? [38] When saw we thee a stranger, and took *thee* in? or naked, and clothed *thee?* [39] Or when saw we thee sick, or in prison, and came unto thee?
>
> [25:40] And the King shall answer and say unto them, Verily I say unto you, Inasmuch as ye have done *it* unto one of the least of these my brethren, ye have done *it* unto me.
>
> [25:41] Then shall he say also unto them on the left hand, Depart from me, ye cursed, into everlasting fire, prepared for the devil and his angels: [42] For I was an hungred, and ye gave me no meat: I was thirsty, and ye gave me no drink: [43] I was a stranger, and ye took me not in: naked, and ye clothed me not: sick, and in prison, and ye visited me not.

[25:44] Then shall they also answer him, saying, Lord, when saw we thee an hungred, or athirst, or a stranger, or naked, or sick, or in prison, and did not minister unto thee?
[25:45] Then shall he answer them, saying, Verily I say unto you, Inasmuch as ye did *it* not to one of the least of these, ye did *it* not to me.
[25:46] And these shall go away into everlasting punishment: but the righteous into life eternal.

Here, Jesus based His criteria for judgment on how His people were treated when they needed help: **"the least of these,** [Christ's] **brethren"** (25:10, 45). It should seem obvious that believers ought to be doing what they can to help out their brothers and sisters in Christ. We know at the outset by His words that whatever we choose to do or not to do, it is ultimately Jesus we either help, or choose not to help. We are children of God, and ambassadors for Christ (1st John 3:1; 2nd Cor. 5:20). As such, we should be looking for opportunities to help others, and particularly our brothers and sisters in Christ, even to **"the least of these"** our brethren.

Galatians 6:10
[6:10] As we have therefore opportunity, let us do good unto all *men,* especially unto them who are of the household of faith.

A Final Note

In this present hour, many if not most churches have departed from the purpose of God in providing for His people. Churches waste millions of dollars on elaborate buildings, sound systems, and a multitude of other things that have nothing to do with the ways of God as revealed in the Scriptures.

Many larger churches provide for their ministers salaries that far exceed the average wages of the people in their congregations, and add to that such luxuries as housing and car allowance, schooling, books, paid travel and more. All the while, people in their congregations whose tithes and offerings go to support these expenses are hurting financially. How can a wealthy preacher even begin to fathom the poverty and struggles his people face in their daily lives when he has everything given to him as on a silver platter, and at their expense? (I write this as a pastor myself.)

In the Old Testament, the tithe was one of several ways God used to provide for those who otherwise could not provide for themselves. The New Testament instructs us to give according to the needs of others when we have the means to do so. When it is God's purpose for His people to see to the needs of one another (John 15:12; 1st John 3:17), and his people are caught up in other things, even to the point of taking from those in need to continue on in these other things, how can we not expect some kind of consequence from God? In His unchanging purpose that we transform into His likeness, where do you stand today? With what teachings have you aligned yourself: the teachings of God, or the doctrines of men?

God does not change. God's purposes do not change. He feeds the birds and clothes the lilies of the field (Matt. 6:26-29). He provides the rain so that we can have food

(Matt. 5:45). It is also God's unchanging purpose that His children take on His character. Yet our current situation has churches facing many expenses that have nothing to do with the ways of God as revealed in the Scriptures. Certainly these things must be addressed in the process of returning to God's principles. So what can we do?

Proverbs 19:17
[19:17] He that hath pity upon the poor lendeth unto the LORD; and that which he hath given will he pay him again.

The most obvious answer to that is to repent. We have gone astray from God's Word, and departed from His instruction. We need to ask His forgiveness and seek His counsel. Churches and individuals have acquired a variety of expenses that need to be handled within the context of each situation. Congregations that have chosen the expense of a building still have building expenses. Pastors and other workers still need to eat. Other financial commitments, such as individual expenses as well as those shared by the church need to be honored.

To maintain (or perhaps restore) the integrity of our identity in Christ, we need to resolve our unnecessary financial commitments previously made with those on the outside in all honesty, and eliminate expenses that are not essential. And for those people who we all know are struggling financially, let's find out ways to help them; in secret. Maybe then the blessings of Malachi 3 and the promises of Jesus regarding the "Father who sees in secret" will begin to flow among God's people.

Appendix

Church Doctrine of Giving:

From Generosity to Mandate

But in vain they do worship me,
teaching *for* doctrines the commandments of men.

Matthew 15:9

Introduction

The Old Testament tithe was for Israel under the Law of Moses. Within that economy, its priests and Levites received regular offerings from the people who worked the land and raised livestock. That economy ended twice: the first time was during the Babylonian captivity, and the other happened in A.D. 70, with the destruction of Jerusalem and its temple. When Israel's economy ended, the tithes and offerings associated with it also ended. No temple, no priesthood. No priesthood, no tithes and offerings.

The priesthood of the New Testament is made up of all believers (1st Peter 2:5, 9; Rev. 1:6). As such, there is no necessity for tithing to priests, for every Christian is a priest of God through Jesus Christ. Certainly we are to support those who minister among us, as well as provide for those in need. We are to give as God gave, or at least reflect His grace in our giving; but nowhere in the New Testament is the Christian commanded to tithe from his or her income on a regular basis for anything. So how did we get to the point where Christians see it as their obligation to do just that?

This appendix has been added to answer that question. Here we will explore the history of Christian giving across the ages. In this survey, we will examine the primary sources from eye witness testimony to get a firsthand look at how Christians initially gave during those early years following the time of the apostles. From these eyewitness accounts, we will see how Christians understood giving in their day, when the teachings of the apostles were still fresh and new, before the corrupt ideas of men began to take hold.

We will also read from the works of some early church leaders during this time period and shortly thereafter. Their ideas on giving and support for the ministry mark the initial stages of man's departure from the Scriptures, which is important to our study because of the shift in authority that took place in the early church. Scriptural authority became secondary as men began to assume leadership positions. Ultimately, the decisions of church councils would become the defining rule for church practice in the form of canon laws.

Moving into the Middle-Ages, we will look at these canon laws, and witness this transition in authority from solid Biblical teaching to the sinking sand of human understanding. By reading the very documents that governed official church policy, we will span over a thousand years of history in a few pages to learn how this authority shift ensnared the very people for whom Christ died to set free. Following its progression into the dawn of modern history, we will observe not only how freewill offerings were transformed to become mandatory tithes, but also how money began to be used as a tithe in the church, how secular government became involved in enforcing tithes, as well as a transition in the recipients of the offerings. Finally, we will learn where all of this ultimately led, to include how the mandatory tithes of England influenced government and church policy in the United States.

The Church Fathers

The Church Fathers are those Christians who arrived on the scene shortly after the completion of the New Testament. The writings of these men provide some insight into the affairs of church life immediately after the time of the apostles.

Justin Martyr (A.D. 110-165)

By A.D. 100, the ministry of Christ's apostles had ended. John, the last of the apostles, departed this life and the churches were in the hands of the next generation of Christians. Justin was born during this generation. He grew up to become a philosopher in search of truth. At some point, he met an old man near the seashore at Ephesus, a Christian. It was through the words of this aged Christian that Justin became convinced of the truth of the gospel, and accepted Christ.[24]

Justin is remembered as one of the first Christian apologists (defenders of the faith). He left us with many of his writings defending Christianity against a world that strongly opposed it. Among his writings is a work entitled *The First Apology of Justin.* This was a defense of Christianity against the Roman worldview. The following is an excerpt from that work, in which Justin described Christian worship. Among the items he described was the practice of Christian giving in his day. As his name implies, Justin was a martyr for Christ. He was beheaded in Rome.[25]

---

[24] Coxe, Cleveland A., D.D., *Ante-Nicene Fathers*, Vol. 1, pp. 195-198. (Hendrickson Publishers, Inc. Peabody, Mass., 1994 reprint of edition by the Christian Literature Publishing Company, 1886).
[25] *Ibid.*, pp. 305-306.

Chap. LXVII. — Weekly Worship of the Christians.[26]

And the wealthy among us help the needy; and we always keep together; and for all things wherewith we are supplied, we bless the Maker of all through His Son Jesus Christ, and through the Holy Ghost. And on the day called Sunday, all who live in cities or in the country gather together to one place, and the memoirs of the apostles or the writings of the prophets are read, as long as time permits; then, when the reader has ceased, the president verbally instructs, and exhorts to the imitation of these good things. Then we all rise together and pray, and, as we before said, when our prayer is ended, bread and wine and water are brought, and the president in like manner offers prayers and thanksgivings, according to his ability, and the people assent, saying Amen; and there is a distribution to each, and a participation of that over which thanks have been given, and to those who are absent a portion is sent by the deacons. And they who are well to do, and willing, give what each thinks fit; and what is collected is deposited with the president, who succours the orphans and widows and those who, through sickness or any other cause, are in want, and those who are in bonds and the strangers sojourning among us, and in a word takes care of all who are in need. But Sunday is the day on which we all hold our common assembly, because it is the first day on which God, having wrought a change in the darkness and matter, made the world; and Jesus Christ our Saviour on the same day rose from the dead. For He was crucified on the day before that of Saturn (Saturday); and on the day after that of Saturn, which is the day of the Sun, having appeared to His apostles and disciples, He taught them these things, which we have submitted to you also for your consideration.

Here, Justin provides a firsthand account of church practice during his years. According to Justin, Christians came together on Sunday, where they learned from the

---

[26] *Ibid.*, p. 186.

Scriptures and were encouraged to put into practice the things they had learned. They prayed together and shared in the Lord's Supper.

On giving, we find that the wealthy were the primary givers, which fits well with the instruction of 1st Tim. 6:17-19. Those who gave are described as **"willing,"** and gave according to their own judgment (**"what each thinks fit"**).[27] What was **"collected"** was used to help **"all who** [were] **in need,"** to include **"orphans and widows,"** adhering well to the Scriptural focus of giving in both Testaments.

There is no compulsory tithe to be found in this testimony of Justin, and collections were used to provide for those in need. Keep in mind that this was only fifty years after the apostolic age, leaving little room for very much change by Justin's time. The New Testament standard for giving, as well as God's unchanging purpose for provision, was still preserved and practiced in the church by A.D. 150.

Tertullian (A.D. 145-220)

Tertullian was born during Justin's lifetime. He lived in Carthage, a city on the Mediterranean coast of Africa. It was Tertullian who first coined the word, "Trinity," which we use to describe the divinity of the Father, Son and Holy Spirit in a single term. The following is from his *Apology*. Like *The First Apology of Justin*, this is another work in defense of Christianity and is well worth reading in its entirety. Tertullian's work is somewhat lengthy in describing a Christian assembly, so we will only focus on his testimony regarding the practice of giving. Here, Tertullian described church life as he experienced it. This

---

[27] Compare 1st Corinthians 9:7. "Every man according as he purposeth in his heart, *so let him give;* not grudgingly, or of necessity: for God loveth a cheerful giver."

is another eyewitness testimony.

Apology, Chap. XXXIX.[28]

The tried men of our elders preside over us, obtaining that honour not by purchase, but by established character. There is no buying and selling of any sort in the things of God. Though we have our treasure-chest, it is not made up of purchase-money, as of a religion that has its price. On the monthly day, if he likes, each puts in a small donation; but only if it be his pleasure, and only if he be able: for there is no compulsion; all is voluntary. These gifts are, as it were, piety's deposit fund. For they are not taken thence and spent on feasts, and drinking-bouts, and eating-houses, but to support and bury poor people, to supply the wants of boys and girls destitute of means and parents, and of old persons confined now to the house; such, too, as have suffered shipwreck; and if there happen to be any in the mines, or banished to the islands, or shut up in the prisons, for nothing but their fidelity to the cause of God's Church, they become the nurslings of their confession.

One in mind and soul, we do not hesitate to share our earthly goods with one another. All things are common among us but our wives.

In writing to the Roman authorities, Tertullian introduces the topic of giving by stating that the leaders in the church did not **"purchase"** their positions[29], but earned them through **"established character."** This statement on purchasing provides the hinge upon which he turns to introduce the topic of **"buying and selling,"** and the use of money in the church.

---

28   *Ante-Nicene Fathers*, Vol. 3, p. 46.
29   Purchase of positions in government was a common practice in ancient times. It became known as Simony in the corrupt Roman Church of the Middle-Ages (after Simon, who tried to purchase the Holy Spirit for money in Acts 8:18-24).

As in the case of Justin Martyr, Tertullian provides a firsthand account of how Christian gave their offerings in the church. Collections were taken on a **"monthly"** basis, and giving was voluntary. It was up to the individual whether he gave anything or not (**"if he likes"**; **"only if it be his pleasure"**; **"there is no compulsion"**; **"all is voluntary"**). The money collected was used to care for the poor, the elderly, the orphans, and others in need. The will of God in providing for the needy had not been lost by Tertullian's time.

At A.D. 200, the New Testament standard for giving is still practiced. There is no mandatory tithe, and provision is geared toward those in need. But as we are about to witness, human wisdom had already begun to weave itself into the fabric of church doctrine.

Irenaeus (A.D. 120-202)

Irenaeus was a disciple of a man named Polycarp, who was a disciple of the apostle John. Born in Smyrna, where Polycarp was bishop, Irenaeus grew up to become a church leader. He was the bishop of a town called Lyons, located in what is now France. The following excerpt is from his work, *Against Heresies.* Unlike the testimonies of Justin and Tertullian, this is not an eyewitness account of church practice in his day. It is merely his commentary on some of the words of Christ, mostly from the Sermon on the Mount. Because Irenaeus was a notable bishop, his written thoughts would greatly influence the mindsets of later church leaders.

Against Heresies, Book 4, Chapter 13[30]

3. And for this reason did the Lord, instead of that [commandment], "Thou shalt not commit adultery," forbid even concupiscence; and instead of that which runs thus,

---

[30] *Ante-Nicene Fathers*, Vol. 1, p. 477.

"Thou shalt not kill," He prohibited anger; and instead of the law enjoining the giving of tithes, [He told us] to share all our possessions with the poor; and not to love our neighbours only, but even our enemies; and not merely to be liberal givers and bestowers, but even that we should present a gratuitous gift to those who take away our goods. For "to him that taketh away thy coat," He says, "give to him thy cloak also; and from him that taketh away thy goods, ask them not again; and as ye would that men should do unto you, do ye unto them:" so that we may not grieve as those who are unwilling to be defrauded, but may rejoice as those who have given willingly, and as rather conferring a favour upon our neighbours than yielding to necessity.
Now all these [precepts], as I have already observed, were not the injunctions of one doing away with the law, but of one fulfilling, extending, and widening it among us; just as if one should say, that the more extensive operation of liberty implies that a more complete subjection and affection towards our Liberator had been implanted within us.

In beginning this section, Irenaeus loosely quoted Jesus, following the Lord's line of reasoning as recorded Matthew's gospel. Let's see how well Irenaeus lines up with Jesus.

Irenaeus:

> *And for this reason did the Lord, instead of that [commandment], "Thou shalt not commit adultery," forbid even concupiscence*

Jesus:

> *Ye have heard that it was said by them of old time, Thou shalt not commit adultery: But I say unto you, That whosoever looketh on a woman to lust after her hath committed adultery with her already in his heart. (Matthew 5:27-28)*

Irenaeus is fairly close to an accurate rendering of Christ's words here. Concupiscence is strong desire, and is normally understood as desire of the sexual variety. His next comparison, however, is not so accurate.

Irenaeus:

> *and instead of that which runs thus, "Thou shalt not kill," He prohibited anger*

Jesus:

> *Ye have heard that it was said by them of old time, Thou shalt not kill; and whosoever shall kill shall be in danger of the judgment: But I say unto you, That whosoever is angry with his brother without a cause shall be in danger of the judgment (Matthew 5:21-22a)*

In this instance, Irenaeus is off target. Irenaeus stated that Jesus prohibited anger altogether. But Jesus did not say that. According to Jesus, it is anger toward a brother without a cause that places one in danger. Scripture does not prohibit anger. Scripture prohibits sin.

Ephesians 4:26

> ***Be ye angry, and sin not:*** *let not the sun go down upon your wrath:*

So here we see that Irenaeus was not accurate in his rendering of the mind of Christ. Next he compares Christian giving with tithing.

Irenaeus:

> *and instead of the law enjoining the giving of tithes, [He told us] to share all our possessions with the poor*

Jesus:

The reason why Jesus' quote is missing here is because Jesus never mentioned the tithe in His teachings on giving. This connection, which is assumed by Irenaeus, does not exist. While Irenaeus was right in regard to the Old Testament use of the tithe, he is out of bounds in making a connection where Jesus does not.

Irenaeus also missed the mark in describing the work of grace in a believer's life. Let's have another look at that final paragraph in the quote.

> Now all these [precepts], as I have already observed, were not the injunctions of one doing away with the law, but of one fulfilling, extending, and widening it among us; just as if one should say, that the more extensive operation of liberty implies that a more complete subjection and affection towards our Liberator had been implanted within us.

Rather than "**doing away with the law**," as Irenaeus tells us, he calls the words of Christ "**injunctions**," meant for "**extending and widening** [the law] **among us**." Here, Irenaeus has moved into doctrinal error of a dangerous kind.

Galatians 3:10-13

[3:10] **For as many as are of the works of the law are under the curse:** *for it is written, Cursed is every one that continueth not in all things which are written in the book of the law to do them. [11] But that no man is justified by the law in the sight of God, it is evident: for, The just shall live by faith. [12]* **And the law is not of faith:** *but, The man that doeth them shall live in them.*
[3:13] Christ hath redeemed us from the curse of the law, being made a curse for us: for it is written, Cursed is every one that hangeth on a tree:

Galatians 5:18

But if ye be led of the Spirit, ye are not under the law.

The work of grace in a believer's heart is not an extension or a widening of the Law, as Irenaeus wrote, but rather an expansion of Christ working in those who have been born from above. It is a spiritual growth that comes only by a spiritual birth. It has nothing to do with the Law, but has everything to do with the Life. By using such phrases as "**extending and widening** [the law] **among us**," and "**the giving of tithes**," it is likely that Irenaeus opened a door of ideas that would influence the direction of later church leaders.

Cyprian (A.D. 200-258)

Cyprian became the bishop of Carthage, where Tertullian had lived. His writings are probably the earliest to date that actually entertain the idea of tithing to church leaders. It is in his *Epistle LXV* that Cyprian specifically connects support for church clergy to the tithe of the Levites.

Epistle LXV[31]

For it is written: "No man that warreth for God entangleth himself with the affairs of this life, that he may please Him to whom he has pledged himself." As this is said of all men, how much rather ought those not to be bound by worldly anxieties and involvements, who, being busied with divine and spiritual things, are not able to withdraw from the Church, and to have leisure for earthly and secular doings! The form of which ordination and engagement the Levites formerly observed under the law ... and received the tithes from the eleven tribes, for their food and maintenance, from the fruits which grew. All which was done by divine authority and arrangement, so that they who waited on divine services might in no respect be called away, nor be compelled to consider or to transact secular business. Which plan and rule is now maintained in respect of the clergy, that they who are promoted by clerical ordination in the Church of the Lord may be called off in no respect from the divine administration, nor be tied down by worldly anxieties and matters; but in the honour of the brethren who contribute, receiving as it were tenths of the fruits, they may not withdraw from the altars and sacrifices, but may serve day and night in heavenly and spiritual things.

Cyprian begins by paraphrasing a passage of Scripture (2nd Timothy 2:4), from which he proceeds to make his point that those in the ministry should not be involved in **"earthly and secular doings."** (He seems to have overlooked the fact that the apostle Paul worked for a

---

[31] *Ibid.*, p. 367.

living as a tentmaker: Acts 18:1-3). He then connects the **"tithes"** received by the **"Levites"** to the contributions received by the **"clergy."** Here Cyprian is completely off base in his understanding of the passage he quoted. The verse has nothing to do with ministerial support, but is rather instructional for Timothy (and all other church leaders) to be committed to the gospel of Jesus Christ. Here is the greater context of 2nd Timothy 2:4.

2nd Timothy 2:1-4

[2:1] Thou therefore, my son, be strong in the grace that is in Christ Jesus. [2] And the things that thou hast heard of me among many witnesses, the same commit thou to faithful men, who shall be able to teach others also.
[2:3] Thou therefore endure hardness, as a good soldier of Jesus Christ.[4] No man that warreth entangleth himself with the affairs of this life; that he may please him who hath chosen him to be a soldier.

Paul instructs Timothy to *"be strong in the grace that is in Christ Jesus"* (2:1). He tells him to *"commit"* the things he heard of Paul *"to faithful men, who shall be able to teach others also"* (2:2). He tells Timothy to *"endure hardness, as a good soldier of Jesus Christ"* (2:3). In verse four, Paul develops this thought by the illustration of the soldier *"that warreth."* A soldier at war does not get involved in the *"affairs of this life, that he may please him who hath chosen him to be a soldier."*

This passage is about pleasing Christ, not sustenance for the ministry. It is about proper focus and endurance in the ministry of the gospel, not how the laity is to support the clergy. So where did Cyprian get his information?

Irenaeus had already made a connection between the Old Testament tithe, and giving according Christ's teachings. It is likely that Cyprian was building on the foundation that Irenaeus had already established. The difference is that while Irenaeus has the poor receiving the offerings, Cyprian has the clergy as the recipients.

Cyprian further states that this is the **"plan and rule now maintained in respect of the clergy**." There is no plan or rule like the one Cyprian describes here to be found anywhere in the New Testament; but Cyprian states that there is one. Perhaps that rule arrived at about the same time as the **"altars and sacrifices"** Cyprian mentioned.[32] There are no altars for sacrifices mentioned in the New Testament in regard to Christian worship. Jesus was the sacrifice to end all sacrifices. As there is no need for further sacrifices, there is no need for the altars on which to perform them.

By A.D. 250, the churches had begun to stray from the truth in regard to giving. While Cyprian did stop short of stating that clergy in his day actually received tithes, the phrase, **"receiving as it were tenths of the fruits,"** denotes a very close comparison. Eventually, as we shall see, the tithe will become the order of the day.

The Constitutions of the Holy Apostles (circa A.D. 250-300[33])

This spurious work was promoted as though it were written by the very apostles themselves. As such, it is a true blemish on Christian history. The Scriptures warned that the false teachers would come.[34] So it is no surprise that false teachers did begin to spread lies with the intent to bring God's people into subjection. The New Testament, as well as the writings of early church leaders contain solid rebuke; exposing certain false teachers, as well as

---

[32] Tertullian and Cyprian are probably the earliest advocates of the Lord's Supper as a sacrifice. See Schaff, Philip, *History of the Christian Church*, Vol. II, pp. 243, 246-247. Charles Scribner's Sons, 1910, reprinted by Eerdmans Publishing Company, Grand Rapids, MI, 1992. Hereafter referred to as *History of the Church*.

[33] *Ante-Nicene Fathers*, Vol. 7, p. 388-389.

[34] Acts 20:28-31; 2nd Corinthians 11:12-15; 1st Timothy 4:1-2; 2nd Peter 2:1

their heretical doctrines that led people astray. Yet this document, a known forgery even in its time, was actually revered and put to use, particularly in the Eastern Church.[35] What had become of church leadership? History has already testified, and it does get worse.

Chapter 25 of Book II is our primary concern as it lays out some specific demands in regard to offerings. Because the chapter is lengthy, only the portions that directly relate to our subject are quoted.

> **Book II Chapter 25: Of First-Fruits and Tithes, etc.** [36]
>
> Let him use those tenths and first-fruits, which are given according to the command of God, as a man of God; as also let him dispense in a right manner the free-will offerings which are brought in on account of the poor, to the orphans, the widows, the afflicted, and strangers in distress, as having that God for the examiner of his accounts who has committed the disposition to him.
>
> You, therefore, O bishops, are to your people priests and Levites, ... You are to the laity prophets, rulers, governors, and kings; the mediators between God and His faithful people, who receive and declare His word, well acquainted with the Scriptures. Ye are the voice of and witnesses of His will, who bear the sins of all, and intercede for all;
>
> As, therefore, you bear the weight, so have you a right to partake of the fruits before others, and to impart to those that are in want, as being to give an account to Him, who without bias will examine your accounts. For those who attend upon the Church ought to be maintained by the Church, as being priests, Levites, presidents, and ministers of God; as it is written in the book of Numbers concerning the priests: "And the Lord said unto Aaron, Thou, and thy sons, and the house of thy family, shall bear the iniquities of the holy things of priesthood."

---

[35] *History of the Church*, Vol. II, pp. 185-186.
[36] *Ibid.*, p. 408.

> Hear this, you of the laity also, the elect Church of God. ...Hear attentively now what was said formerly: oblations and tithes belong to Christ our High Priest, and to those who minister to Him. Tenths of salvation are the first letter of the name of Jesus. ...Those which were then the sacrifices now are prayers, and intercessions, and thanksgivings. Those which were then first-fruits, and tithes, and offerings, and gifts, now are oblations, which are presented by holy bishops to the Lord God, through Jesus Christ, who has died for them. For these are your high priests, as the presbyters are your priests, and your present deacons instead of your Levites; as are also your readers, your singers, your porters, your deaconesses, your widows, your virgins, and your orphans: but He who is above all these is the High Priest.

Without question there is much that is wrong in the statements above. The development of a clerical hierarchy as rulers ("**rulers, governors, and kings**") with the laity in subjection is diametrically opposed to the words of Jesus Christ, who emphatically stated that the greatest among His disciples were to be as servants (Matthew 23:11).

Here the "**holy bishops**" are the "**high priests**," while the "**presbyters**" are the "**priests**," and the "**deacons**" are "**Levites.**" This is in blatant opposition to Scripture, which acknowledges a priesthood of all believers (1st Peter 2:5, 9). The use of the book of Numbers to transform bishops and deacons into priests and Levites finds no parallel in the New Testament. In fact, the New Testament book of Galatians warns of the danger of mixing Law with Grace (Gal. 3:9-10, 12; 5:1-4). The book of Romans also tells us that Christians are not under the Law (Rom. 6:14; 7:1-4). Today, hindsight reveals where this ultimately led, and history is filled with atrocities committed in the name of Christ by the medieval Catholic Church.

It appears from the opening statement that the church leaders (or "**man of God**," as the text has it) were to receive "**tenths and firstfruits**," while the "**freewill offerings**," were to be distributed to those in need ("**the poor, to the orphans, widows**," etc.). To justify this claim for receiving the goods of others, it is explained that the church leaders are "**mediators between God and his faithful people**," and that they "**bear the weight**," and therefore have "**a right to partake of the fruits before others**." For Scriptural authority, appeal is made to "**the book of Numbers**," and specifically to Aaron and his sons, whom the LORD had appointed to "**bear the iniquities of the holy things of the priesthood**."[37]

Of course, on this side of the cross the book of Numbers does not apply. Outside of Israel, on either side of the cross, the book of Numbers never applied. Nor are church leaders the "**mediators between God and his faithful people**," for there is only "one mediator between God and men, the man Christ Jesus" (2nd Timothy 2:5), who also bore all our iniquities.

While the *Constitutions* never became established as a final authority in the church, they were put to use, and referred to as authoritative in some of the church's decisions.[38] It was preserved as a document of the church, and we shall see its influence in some of the canons of the church councils.

In A.D. 692, the *Constitutions* would finally be rejected by the Second Council of Trullan for its heretical teachings.[39] But by that time, the damage was already done; for in the year 585, at the Second Council of Macon, the tithe was incorporated into the canon laws of the church.

---

[37] Probably a loose quotation from Numbers 18:1.
[38] *History of the Church*, Vol. II, p. 186.
[39] *Ibid.*, p. 186

The Canons of the Church

This section contains some of the decisions made by various church councils throughout the Middle-Ages. The laws decided upon at these councils (or synods) were spelled out in what are called canons, and became official church dogma. These canon laws were held to be authoritative, and were expected to be obeyed. Because the council meetings took place at different localities and were chaired by local church authorities, it is not uncommon for decisions made in one region to differ from those made in another. Most of the canons listed here took place in Gaul, which later became what is now France.

The Synod of Angers: A.D. 453[40]

This synod took place in what is now France. While the tithe is not mentioned in this canon, there is a hint of Cyprian's influence, or that of the *Constitutions of the Holy Apostles.* In only four words, it speaks volumes.

Canon 2
2. Deacons must honour priests.

Here we have a rule not found in the Bible. Yet we have seen that both Cyprian and the *Constitutions* have statements that would lead to the development of such a rule. According to Numbers (18:26-32), the Levites were to give a tenth of the tithes to the priests. In this canon, deacons (which the *Constitutions* equated to Levites) are told that they must honor (provide for) the presbyters (called **"priests"** here).

---

[40] Hefele, Charles J. D.D., *A History of the Councils of the Church from the Original Documents.* Vol. IV, A.D. 451 to A.D. 680, pp. 3-4. Charles Scribner's Sons, New York, 1895. Hereafter referred to as *History of Councils.*

The First Irish Synod: A.D. 450-456 (approximate)[41]

This Irish synod, under St. Patrick, took place at about the same time as the Synod of Angers. Canons 12 and 13 of this synod mention alms. While these are direct references to giving, there is nothing in this synod about tithing.

> **Canon 12**
> No alms shall be received from an excommunicated person.

> **Canon 13**
> The Church must receive no alms from a heathen.

There is something noble about not accepting gifts from certain entities, and reveals a high standard. Yet churches today receive money in their offering plates from whoever happens to be sitting in the pews, including non-members, no questions asked.

The First Council of Tours: November 461

The city of Tours is in France, about fifty miles west of Angers, where the synod of 453 was held. This canon is included because of its use of the phrase, "**priests and Levites**," the same terms found in the *Constitutions of the Holy Apostles* in referring to deacons and presbyters.

> **Canon 1**[42]
> **Priests and Levites are exhorted to perpetual chastity, because they may at any moment be summoned to the discharge of a sacred function.**

While this canon does not mention the tithe, it does demonstrate the human tendency toward control over others. Here, those who minister in the name of Christ

---

41   *Ibid.*, pp. 7-8.
42   *Ibid.*, p. 10.

are subjected to the unscriptural doctrine of celibacy;[43] for even the priests and Levites of the Old Testament had wives.

Synod at Adge: A.D. 506[44]

Adge is located on France's Mediterranean coast. Two of its canons discuss gifts, and sought to address the problem of covetousness.

> **Canon 4**
> **Clerics and laymen who take back presents made to the Church or to a monastery by their ancestors or themselves, shall be excommunicated as murderers of the poor.**
>
> **Canon 6**
> **What is left or presented to a bishop, whether to him and the Church alike or to him alone, belongs, not to the bishop as personal property, but is the property of the Church;**

Apparently some who gave gifts to the ministry had changed their minds, and wanted to take back what had been given. Canon 4 was written to discourage that. However, a problem arises on the issue of ancestors and the rightful inheritance of their descendants. Here the church may be guilty of infringing upon the God-given rights of families to care for their own.[45]

Canon 6 deals with covetousness on the receiving end (the clergy). This manifested itself through bishops who felt that they might keep for themselves items that were offered to the Church. But covetousness is also found on the part of this particular church council, which would take that which is **"presented to a bishop,"** and even what was given to **"him alone."**

---

43   See 1st Timothy 4:1-3.
44   *History of Councils*, pp. 77-78.
45   Proverbs 13:22

In both cases, these canons are a far cry from Him who said:

Luke 6:30
Give to every man that asketh of thee; and of him that taketh away thy goods ask them not again.

Luke 6:35
..., and lend, hoping for nothing again; and your reward shall be great, and ye shall be the children of the Highest: for he is kind unto the unthankful and to the evil.

Of particular interest to this study is the word, **"presents"** (Canon 4). The offerings were called presents. As late as A.D. 506, it was understood that gifts entrusted to representatives of the church were precisely that: gifts. It is also noteworthy that these gifts were to be used to help the **"poor."** Even at this point in the departure from the original truth of Scripture, there was maintained a proper understanding in regard to the gifts and the recipients; and no mandatory tithe will be found in the canons of this synod.

The First Synod of Orleans: A.D. 511

The town of Orleans is located in France about seventy-five miles northeast of Tours. Canon 5 of this synod discusses gifts granted by the King, and how they were to be used.

> **Canon 5**[46]
> **The products of gifts and fields granted by the King to the Church, together with the immunity of the clergy, shall be expended on the repairs of churches, the maintenance of the clergy and the poor, or for the redemption of prisoners.**

---

46 *Ibid.*, p. 89.

Here the offering by the King is called a grant: **"granted by the King."** Important to our study are the recipients of the grant: along with church repairs, the gifts were to be used to provide for clergy and the poor, and to redeem prisoners. There is no mention of a tithe in the canons of this synod.

Synod at Dovin: A.D. 527[47]

This synod took place in Armenia. Several of its canons deal with giving. The offerings are called gifts, and these canons discuss how the gifts are to be received and distributed. Canon 23 has something called *Agape*, which was for the poor. At this synod we also learn that priests were commanded to slay the animals that were given as sacrifices of compassion (Canons 27 and 28).

> Canon 1
> Gifts for priests must be brought into the church, and not into the house of any priest.
>
> Canon 2
> The priests must receive these gifts without selfishness at the sacrifice of the Mass.
>
> Canon 14
> The gifts of the church shall be distributed according to a rule. Priests shall have two parts, deacons a part and a half, the inferiors of the Church and widows (if they are needy) one part.
>
> Canon 23
> The Agape destined for the poor may not be given away by the priests at their pleasure, but must be divided immediately among the poor in the presence of the givers.
>
> Canon 27
> Priests must not at their own pleasure select the cattle which shall be given as sacrifices of compassion (for the clergy and the poor).

47   *Ibid.* pp. 145-147

Canon 28
When such animals are presented, the priest must not keep them living, but must slay them, and divide them among the poor.

We are now at A.D. 527, and have yet to find a mandatory tithe in any official church canon. We read of gifts, presents, grants, and alms, and comparisons to the tithe, but no tithe. And what we do find is that the gifts, presents, grants and alms were to be used to help those in need.

Up to this point, church leaders had invented a lot of unscriptural ideas and made them into canon laws. But they did not forget how to use the gifts they received. Their leaders, as well as the needy among them, were supported by the offerings from the assembly. While our generation may scrutinize them in regard to their church practices and politics, they might well stand up in judgment against churches of our day for their misuse of offerings and neglect of their poor (see Matt. 12:41-42).

The Fourth Synod of Orleans: A.D. 541

Like Canon 4 from the synod at Adge thirty-five years prior, these two canons concern the inheritance of goods or property that has been promised to the Church.[48]

Canon 14
Anything bequeathed to a church or to a bishop by a valid document must not be withheld by the heirs.

Canon 19
If anyone has demonstrably presented anything to the Church in goods or vineyards, even without a written document, neither he nor his heir must reclaim it from the Church, under pain of excommunication.

---

[48] *Ibid.*, p. 212.

These canons were added to address situations in which items promised to the Church were also understood to belong to a family heir. This is a tragic departure from the commandments of Jesus Christ by those who bear His name.

Matthew 5:40

And if any man will sue thee at the law, and take away thy coat, let him have thy cloke also.

Matthew 5:42

Give to him that asketh thee, and from him that would borrow of thee turn not thou away.

Rather than giving to those who would sue for possession, this council maintained church ownership. Rather than taking a higher road in a misunderstanding and suffering loss for the sake of Christ, the church leaders of this council chose a path of covetousness and gain to the loss of others.

The Second Council of Tours: A.D. 567

The Second Council of Tours has been cited as the first time tithing was recommended into church practice.[49] The following is the official statement of that council in regard to giving.

> **Canon 5**[50]
> **Every community shall support its poor, and the poor shall not wander about in strange cities.**

While this is a church mandate for communities to provide for their needy, it is at once dismissed as a recommendation for introducing the tithe, as the tithe is not even mentioned. However, at about this time, there was an authoritative letter addressed to the Christian laity, signed by four of the bishops who were members of

---

[49] *Schaff-Herzog*, Vol. IV, p. 2365.
[50] *History of Councils*, p. 390.

this synod at Tours. The following account describes the discovery of that letter by the Jesuit Jacques Sirmond (1559-1651), which also contains a description of its contents. Among the items addressed is a command to pay the tithe.

> The Jesuit Sirmond recovered, from several MSS, a letter addressed to the Christian laity, either during the second Synod of Tours, or shortly after it (as the superscription says), by four bishops who were members of that synod, particularly Archbishop Euphronius of Tours. In this letter they summon the faithful to penitence and amendment, that they may escape the divine judgment which lies before them. The betrothed should put off their marriage, partly that by prayer and chastity they may propitiate God, partly that, if they should perish in the misery lying before them, they may be cut off with a pure soul. **From all property the tithe must be certainly be paid, even every tenth slave**, and so for every son the third of a pound must be given to the bishops for the redemption of prisoners. Enmities must be laid aside, and incestuous unions dissolved.[51]

From the wording it appears that there may have been some disagreement on this idea of tithing, for which this letter seems to provide an authoritative answer: **"From all property the tithe must certainly be paid."** It is possible that people either were not tithing, or if they were, they were doing so reluctantly. It is probable that the tithe was not yet understood to be compulsory, for up to this point there is no canon from any known church council requiring the tithe. This is the earliest known writing by church leaders in which a mandatory tithe is expected in the church, even to **"every tenth slave."**

---

[51]   *Ibid.*, p. 394

Second Council of Macon: A.D. 585

About two hundred miles southeast of Tours is a town called Macon. It is here, in the Second Council of Macon, that we find the tithe included in its canons.

> **Canon 5**[52]
> **The old law, to pay tithes to the church, is widely neglected, and must therefore be enjoined afresh. The tithe is to be expended for the use of the poor (also of the clergy), and for the redemption of prisoners. Whoever obstinately refuses it is forever excommunicated.**

This is the earliest known canon of a church council mandating the tithe. While it is called the "**old law**" here, it is not clear whether this is a reference to the Old Testament, or some other law (perhaps the *Constitutions of the Holy Apostles*). While the council was certainly wrong in imposing the Law (the Old Testament tithe) onto fellow believers, it is interesting that even as late as A.D. 585, it maintained a Biblical understanding as to how the gifts were to be distributed: "**to be expended for the use of the poor (also of the clergy)**".

The Synod of Rouen

Rouen is in France, about 125 miles north of Orleans. The date of this council is uncertain. Its sixteen canons are variously dated depending on their topics. Most give it a date of A.D. 650. [53]

> **Canon 3**
> **If anyone does not give tithes of all fruits, of oxen, sheep, goats, after being thrice admonished, he is to be anathematized.**

---

52   *Ibid.*, p. 407
53   *Ibid.*, p. 468

By the time of the synod of Rouen, the tithe was an established doctrine. It had been canonized at the Second Council of Macon, and this canon adds another level of condemnation upon those who refuse to submit. These people were not only excommunicated, but they were to be accursed as well. This tightening of rules is a good indication that people were not following them very well. Before long, the government will be involved and people will have things taken from them by force. Note that the tithes still consisted of produce and livestock, and not money.

Provincial Synod of Lusitania (held at Merida): A.D. 666[54]

This synod was held in Spain, and does not discuss the tithe. Canon 14 discusses money that is offered to the church, which is of interest because later on the tithe will include money.

> **Canon 14**
> **That which is offered in money in a cathedral church on a feast day shall be divided into three parts; and one part shall belong to the bishop, a second to the priests and deacons, and the third to the remaining clerics. Similarly, the clergy in the rural churches shall share.**

Apparently some members of the clergy had received an offering of money on a feast day in a cathedral church and did not know what to do about it. So the question was put to the council, and the decision was finalized in this particular canon. Money that is offered in a cathedral on a feast day is to be divided according to the instructions here. We can only wonder how money offered anywhere else on an average day was to be handled. There are probably canons for those situations as well.

---

54 *Ibid.*, p. 483

For our study, it is noteworthy that this council identifies money as an offering in and of itself, and not included as part of the tithe. According to the synod at Rouen, the tithe consisted of "fruits, oxen, sheep, and goats." Also note the recipients. The money offered to the church, according to this synod, was to be divided among the church leaders. Nothing is mentioned in regard to the poor.

The Tithe Established

By the middle of the seventh century, the tithe had been established as canonical in France by at least two church councils and one authoritative letter. Following its progress into England, we may gain some insight into its later development, which also affected church practice here in the United States.

Bishop Eadbert, A.D. 688

Not long after the synod at Lusitania, an account written in A.D. 688 tells of a certain Bishop Eadbert, who lived north of England.

> "[Eadbert was] **a man remarkable for his knowledge of the Scriptures and his observance of the divine commandments, and (most of all) for his alms deeds, which were such that, in every year, he gave to the poor a tithe, not only of his beasts, but of all his corn and fruits of trees, and of his garments also, according to the law.**"[55]

Here we find a bishop who gave an annual "**tithe**" to the "**poor.**" This is indeed "**remarkable**," for in our day and age, the situation is reversed; and tithing from the poor to the church is expected, not yearly, but on a weekly basis. Note that Eadbert was also "**remarkable**" for "**his observance of the divine commandments.**" While this probably refers to the Old Testament Law (note the last statement, "**according to the law**"), the decrees of the Church were also believed to be divine commands. But the fact that he stands out for observing them is noteworthy, and indicates that many in his day were probably not.

---

[55] *The Sacred Tenth*, p.249

King Ethelwulf, A.D. 854

The story of King Ethelwulf comes to us from ninth century Britain. Troubled by Viking invasions, Ethelwulf sought to purchase God's favor in hopes to obtain divine help during a time of distress.

> **"I, Ethelwulf, King of the West Saxons, by the advice of my bishops and other chief men of my kingdom, have resolved on a wholesome and uniform remedy, that is, that I grant as an offering unto God, and the Blessed Virgin, and all the saints, a certain portion of my kingdom to be held by perpetual right, that is to say, the tenth part thereof; and that this tenth part be privileged from temporal duties and free from all secular services and royal tributes ..., for the health of my soul, and the pardon of my sins, to be applied only to the service of God alone, ..."**[56]

King Ethelwulf's reasoning for handing over a tenth of his kingdom should lead one to question the integrity of those bishops that advised him. If Ethelwulf had accepted Christ, his **"sins"** were forgiven. And if that were the case, there was no need for concern over the **"health of his soul."** The fact that **"the Blessed Virgin, and all the saints"** are placed alongside God as recipients of his offering provides evidence as to how far from the Truth the Church had fallen.

From the Tenth to the Sixteenth Century

In A.D 944, a King Edmund held a *witan* (council) in London, which passed a law commanding "every man in the kingdom, upon his Christianity (that is, unless he would be counted a heathen) to pay his tithes...; those neglecting so to do being declared excommunicated."[57]

---

[56] *Ibid.*, pp. 256-257
[57] *Ibid.*, p. 262

In 967, under King Edgar (son of King Edmund), several tithe laws were passed, along with a penalty for those who chose not to obey.

> If any failed to pay tithes, the king's officer, the bishop, and the parish priest were to assemble, to take from the offender the tithe due to the church to which it belonged, to give another tenth to the offender himself (who had kept back his tithe); the remaining parts being forfeited and equally divided between the king's officer and bishop, it being provided that no man should herein be spared, were he the king's tenant, or a lord's.[58]

In 1012, a law under King Ethelred II demanded that "every thane [that is, a landowner] tithe whatever he possesseth...."[59] The definition of the phrase, "whatever he possesseth," is unclear, and can be interpreted in a variety of ways. But money in lieu of tithed livestock can be found by A.D. 1050, in which a law in England, under Edward the Confessor, allowed for a penny for those who only owned "a calf or two."[60]

By this time the tithe had become the law of the land by the authority of secular kings. The tithe had also progressed well beyond produce and livestock, and included a tenth of one's income. Under Edward VI (1537-1553), an Act was passed demanding that "every person exercising merchandise, handicraft, or other art or faculty... shall yearly, at or before the Feast of Easter, pay for his personal tithes the tenth part of his personal gains; ...."[61]

---

[58] *Ibid.*, p. 262
[59] *Ibid.*, p.264
[60] *Ibid.*, 265-266
[61] *Ibid.*, 279-281

From Then Until Now

Later developments in tithing are in part responsible for the reasoning behind the First Amendment of the United States Constitution, which expressly forbids Congress from establishing a national church. Many of the early settlers who came to America from England did so to gain freedom of worship. In their own colonies on this side of the Atlantic, they were free from government enforced tithing to the Church of England; but the colonists in America continued the practice by mandating tithes for the established churches in the colonies. [62]

After the War for Independence, the Founding Fathers chose not to recognize a state religion. Unlike the Church of England, churches here in the United States would not receive tithes in the form of a government imposed tax. Churches did, however, continue the tithe doctrine, as incorporated into the denominations of today. Thus, the tithe as we have it today did not originate in the Bible, but in the traditions of men.

---

[62] The Westchester County Chamber of Commerce, *Tax Exemptions on Real Estate, an Increasing Menace*, White Plains, NY: 1922, pp. 74-77.

Bibliography

Atkerson, Steve, ed. *ekklesia: To the Roots of Biblical Church Life,* Atlanta: New Testament Restoration Foundation, 2003.

Benton, William, Publisher. *Encyclopaedia Britannica*, Vol. 22, Chicago: Encyclopaedia Britannica, Inc., 1959

Bromiley, Geoffery W., General Editor. *The International Standard Bible Encyclopedia*, Volume Four, Q-Z, Grand Rapids: William B. Eerdmans Publishing Company, 1988.

Brown, Francis, D.D., D.Litt., *The Brown-Driver-Briggs Hebrew and English Lexicon*, Peabody, MA: Hendrickson Publishers, Inc., 2000. (Reprinted from the 1906 edition originally published by the Houghlin, Mifflin and Company, Boston.)

Coxe, Cleveland A., D.D., *Ante-Nicene Fathers*, Peabody, MA: Hendrickson Publishers, Inc., 1994.

Criswell, W. A. Ph. D., ed., *The Believer's Study Bible*, Nashville: Thomas Nelson Publishers, 1991.

Gesenius, H.W.F., *Gesenius' Hebrew-Chaldee Lexicon to the Old Testament*, Grand Rapids: Baker Book House, 1979.

Gonzalez, Justo L., *The Story of Christianity*, Vol. 1. New York: Harper Collins, 1984.

Harris, R. Laird; Archer, Gleason L., Jr.; and Waltke, Bruce K., *Theological Wordbook of the Old Testament*, Vol. 1, Chicago: Moody Bible Institute, 1980.

Hefele, Charles J., D.D., *A History of the Councils of the Church from the Original Documents*, Vol. IV, A.D.451-A.D. 680, New York: Charles Scribner's Sons, 1895. (Courtesy of Google books: http://books.google.com)

Josephus, Flavius, *The Works of Josephus*, translated by William Whiston, Peabody, MA: Hendrickson Publishers, Inc., 1987.

Lansdell, Henry, D.D., *The Sacred Tenth, or Studies in Tithe-Giving, Ancient and Modern*, New York: 1906. (Google books)

McGee, J. Vernon, *Through the Bible with J. Vernon McGee*, Vol. 5. Pasadena: Through the Bible Radio, 1983.

Meyers, Rick, *e-Sword – the Sword of the LORD with an electronic edge*, Version 9.5.1, Franklin, TN: 2000-2009 (www.e-sword.net)

Mirehouse, John, *A Practical Treatise on the Law of Tithes*, London: 1822. (Google books)

Schaff, Philip, *History of the Christian Church*, Grand Rapids: Eerdmans Publishing Company, 1992 (reprint from Charles Scribner's Sons, 1910).

Schaff, Philip, ed., *Schaff-Herzog Encyclopaedia of Religious Knowledge*, New York: Funk & Wagnalls Co., 1891.

Tenney, Merrill C., ed., *The Pictorial Bible Dictionary*, Grand Rapids: Zondervan Publishing House, 1968.

Tenney, Merrill C., General Editor, *The Pictorial Encyclopedia of the Bible*, Vol. 5, Q-Z, Grand Rapids: Zondervan, 1975, 1976.

Vine, W. F.: *Vine's Expository Dictionary of New Testament Words*, Oliphants, Ltd., 1952.

Walvoord John F. and Zuck, Roy B., eds., *The Bible Knowledge Commentary: Old Testament*, Wheaton, IL: Victor Books, 1985.

Westchester County Chamber of Commerce, *Tax Exemptions on Real Estate: an Increasing Menace*, White Plains, NY: 1922 (Google books)

Wilson, William, *Wilson's Old Testament Word Studies*, Peabody, MA: Hendrickson Publishers

www.ingramcontent.com/pod-product-compliance
Lightning Source LLC
Chambersburg PA
CBHW060755050426
42449CB00008B/1412